Death's Code Bible

DEATH'S CODE BIBLE

STEVE CANADA

authorHOUSE®

AuthorHouse™ LLC
1663 Liberty Drive
Bloomington, IN 47403
www.authorhouse.com
Phone: 1-800-839-8640

Published by AuthorHouse   08/30/2013

ISBN: 978-1-4918-0612-8 (sc)
ISBN: 978-1-4918-0611-1 (e)

Library of Congress Control Number: 2013914269

Contents

Preface

Death rears its ugly head everywhere and at all times, in all sorts of situations and under many kinds of circumstances and from a myriad of reasons, affecting people in surprising ways, but eventually coming for everyone no matter their station in life. But why do we find their demises encoded in the Five Books of Moses? What is it about a sacred text of 304,805 Hebrew letters that enables it to hold the whole history of humankind, and encoded within it the specific circumstances under which particular people are going to die? Connected to the types of events listed below are found the names of those who died in instances of those particular events (see Book List at end of this book), such as the Titanic's sinking in 1912, the tornado in Moore, Oklahoma in 2013, and in Joplin, Missouri, and the Sandy Hook School Shooting in 2012.

Titanic, crash, ice, sunk, dead, April, 1912, Atlantic; from Genesis 40:17 to Leviticus 21:5; skip 5858 letters to find the Key, 'Titanic,' encoded. All the names of the dead from this tragic accident are found in this *one* Torah Matrix; see Book List for ordering information.

NaziShoah [holocaust], **'Aushvitz,' camp, hanged, torture, kill, gas, annihilation, genocide**; from Genesis 1:1 to Leviticus 8:12; skip 8303 letters to find the Key, 'NaziShoah.' All victims' names searched for so far are found encoded in this *one* Torah Matrix; see Book List for ordering information. At one name per page it would take millions of pages to show all encoded.

AuroraCO, July 20, 2012, shooting, Dark, Knight, Risen, Jim, H(o)lm(e)s, killing, homicide, murderer; from Genesis 1:1 to Deuteronomy 31:8, skip 19,376 letters to find the Key encoded; all victims' names of this mass shooting are found encoded in two Torah Matrices; see Book List for ordering information.

Fukushima, ['nuke, power, electric' found encoded in another Matrix], **March 11, 2011, core, melted, poison, escaped**; from Numbers 19:14 to Deuteronomy 14:21; skip 2669 letters to find the Key, 'Fukushima,' encoded. Not all victims' names are known; see Book List.

Hurricane, Florida, 1960, Donna, USA; from Genesis 1:24 to Deut. 12:16, skip 13,601 letters to find the Key encoded. Also **Miami, Keys, 1919,** and **Carolina, New, York.**

Tornado, Joplin, Miz-ouri, death, May; from Gen. 1:1 to Deut. 21:14, skip 21,000 letters to find the Key, 'Tornado,' encoded. Also **Moore, Okla-homa, USA, May.**

Benghazi, killing, weapons, death, USA, murder, shooting, army/warfare, jihad; from Genesis 1:1 to 2 Samuel 20:22, skip 32,613 letters to find the Key encoded. Same terms found encoded also from Gen. 1:1 to 2 Kings 22:9, skip 39,055 letters to find the Key encoded. Clarity through redundancy is a hallmark of these Torah composers, encoders and communicators.

Bos(ton)Marath(on), Boston, Mass., Mara-thon, bomb, pressure, cooker, terror; from Exodus 5:2 to 1 Samuel 9:16, skip 15,715 letters to find Key encoded; [+ the two bombers' names, their ethnic origin, and all dead victims, and 'Boylston Street'].

B.Marathon, evildoer, crime, evil, terror, terrorist; from Gen. 15:1 to Numbers 2:1, skip 8638 letters to find Key encoded. [+ the 2 bombers' names, and all dead victims, 'Boylston Street']

Hiroshima, Japan, August 6, 1945, nuke, weapons, USA; from Exodus 9:21 to Leviticus 11:6, skip 3274 letters to find Key encoded, in Matrix 6 of 12 found of key. **Honshu, destroyed, death, 'tomic, destruction, B-29, Tinian, Enola, Gay**; found in Matrix 7 of 12; (pilot's name also found encoded, and the bomb's name). Victims' names are not available; also for Nagasaki.

Nagasaki, Japan, August 9, 1945, nuke, 'tomic, weapons; from Gen. 1:1 to Deut. 16:22, skip 14,119 letters to find Key encoded, in Matrix 2 of 2. **Nuke, Fat, Man, uran-ium, B-29** in Matrix 1 of 2 found of the Key; (pilot and plane's name also found encoded).

credit: L. Jamison

Steve Canada

Introduction

"The only new thing in this world is the history you don't know." Harry Truman

Chapters in this book are only representative samples from much larger, full-length Reports or whole Books on those subjects—available for ordering directly from the author—see Book List at end of this book. These are hand-made Reports and Books produced by the author; in these are shown the names of the dead from each circumstance as encoded in the Torah.

The Bible is encoded with many interesting names and phrases, some apparently predictive of historical events. These are discovered by counting any certain number of letters, that is, 'skipping' any chosen number of letters (ELS . . . Equidistant Letter Sequence) starting from anywhere in the original Hebrew text.

Code searchers usually restrict their work to the Torah, the first five books of the Bible; others use what Christians call the whole 'Old Testament.' It is recommended to read R. Edwin Sherman's 2004 book *Bible Code Bombshell*. He is a mathematician and eschews sensationalistic approaches to Bible Code discoveries. He is the founder of the 'Isaac Newton Bible Code Research Society,' located in southern Oregon; free membership and newsletter on website www.biblecodedigest.com.

Death's Bible Code: Names of the Dead Throughout History are found encoded in the Torah, the Five Books of Moses. From Ancient Egypt to Auschwitz to the Titanic to Sandy Hook Mass Shooting to Boston Marathon Bombing, all the dead's names are found encoded. Assassinations over 4000 years, casualties of wars, accidents, mass shootings, natural disasters, and terror attacks—their names are found secretly encoded in the sacred Word of Yahweh, *with* the name of the event in which they died.

"Don't be afraid to see what you see." Ronald Reagan

The embedded Torah information is clear, conspicuous and concise. The original Hebrew text seen in the chapters and sections in this book has not been changed even by *one* letter in about 3400 years, since the time Yahweh dictated it letter-by-letter to Moses on Mt. Sinai. I don't know precisely who composed and the dictated Torah, or how much care, effort, time, resources or editing went into its design or code architecture, but given what has been uncovered in the plain text just by counting between letters during the past 900 years of Bible Code study, the nature of the intelligence behind it is consistent with what is known elsewhere about the identity and abilities of Yahweh (see Sitchin in References).

Search for terms entered is done automatically by the Bible Code program (for example, *Bible Code Plus*, from Israel via USPS). Search is done forward, then backward, through the whole Torah (or within any range you specify); any spelling direction found is valid, be it horizontal, vertical or diagonal. No knowledge of any Hebrew is needed in order to do Bible Code research. Search terms can be entered using the program's dictionary or lexicon or 'dates' list, or entered phonetically using transliteration (letter-by-letter, sound for corresponding sound from English to Hebrew using the program's on-screen keyboard).

The first term the program will search for is the 'Key,' and if found encoded it will stand vertically with letters touching in correct spelling sequence, either top-to-bottom or the reverse. Any spelling direction of any term found encoded is a valid search result. For example, enter the Key as 'Titanic,' transliterated with Hebrew letter sounds, and only *one* such encoded word is found in the whole Torah, in *one* Matrix. Up to six terms can be searched for at the same time, along with the Key. All factors about that disastrous iceberg crash and sinking are found encoded in that *one* Matrix, along with *all* the names of those who died that fateful night (see Book List).

'Proximity' means the visual distance between the Key Code and any other code or word in the retrieved matrix. Bible Code research theory states that the closer the pairings are, i.e., the more compact the visual cluster effect, the greater their significance. Jeffrey Satinover, MD, in his book *Cracking the Bible Code*, says "there is a tendency for meaningfully related words to show the cluster effect, appearing in the array more closely together than unrelated words." (Quoted in manual that comes with the *Bible Codes Plus* computer disc, p.9).

The odds of the Key in any particular Matrix being found encoded by chance can go as low as one in a million or less as calculated automatically by the *Bible Code Plus* computer program (available directly from Israel). While the odds could be even lower than that, the program does not calculate below that. The encodement algorithm used by the Torah composers that allows such dense search results of the encoded found terms (whether in syllables or not) encoded so close to the Key (see 'Proximity' note elsewhere) and to each other, is a function of an unknown technology and encryption mathematics.

The essential sounds that comprise the encoded words are phonetically rendered coherent, readable and understandable through transliteration, finding the equivalent sound of the English letter in the appropriate, corresponding Hebrew letter that has the same sound as shown in the on-screen keyboard . . . those strung together in correct spelling sequence, keeps the English sound of the word entered in the search function of the program; for example, 'Titanic' or 'Concordia.'

The Torah Code matrices shown in this short book in the following pages are representative selections from longer, individual books on those subjects of the 8 Parts of this book. See Books and Reports List at end, for titles, page count, prices and ordering information.

Part 1 Accidents

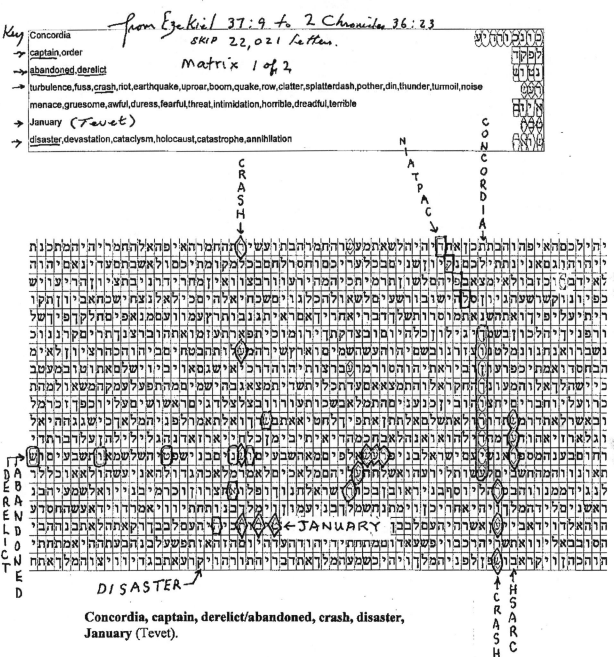

Concordia, captain, derelict/abandoned, crash, disaster, January (Tevet).

Note lower left where three encoded words touch each other (horizontal 'abandoned,' vertical 'crash', and diagonal 'disaster'). This type of extremely close encoding reveals intimate historical connections, as shown by the tragic event of January 13, 2012 off the coast of Giglio Island, off the west coast of Italy, opposite the Tuscan region (these specific terms were not found encoded with this Key word at its maximum search skip; perhaps with other spelling variations they might be found encoded).

Titanic

(No Part B)

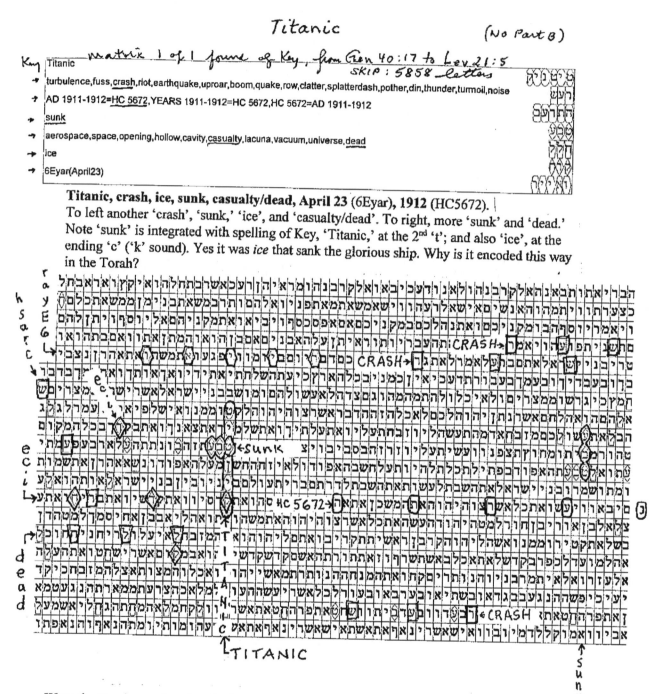

Key — Titanic — matrix 1 of 1 found of Key, from Gen 40:17 to Lev 21:5 SKIP: 5858 letters

turbulence,fuss,crash,riot,earthquake,uproar,boom,quake,row,clatter,splatterdash,pother,din,thunder,turmoil,noise

AD 1911-1912=HC 5672,YEARS 1911-1912=HC 5672,HC 5672=AD 1911-1912

sunk

aerospace,space,opening,hollow,cavity,casualty,lacuna,vacuum,universe,dead

ice

6Eyar(April23)

Titanic, crash, ice, sunk, casualty/dead, April 23 (6Eyar), 1912 (HC5672).
To left another 'crash', 'sunk,' 'ice', and 'casualty/dead'. To right, more 'sunk' and 'dead.'
Note 'sunk' is integrated with spelling of Key, 'Titanic,' at the 2nd 't'; and also 'ice', at the
ending 'c' ('k' sound). Yes it was *ice* that sank the glorious ship. Why is it encoded this way
in the Torah?

Were the Torah encoders "predicting" the disaster, or somehow foretelling what would occur,
depending on who was in "control" of events?
The correct year (HC5672, the first part of 1912, according to the lunar calendar used by the
Hebrews) is found encoded to the right of the Key, 'Titanic,'
While only April 23 ('6Eyar' in the Hebrew calendar) was found encoded as the closest date to
the April 15 sinking disaster, it is only 8 days from the sinking, about 3 a.m.. No date from April
8 to 22, or from 24 to 27 was found encoded with this Key.

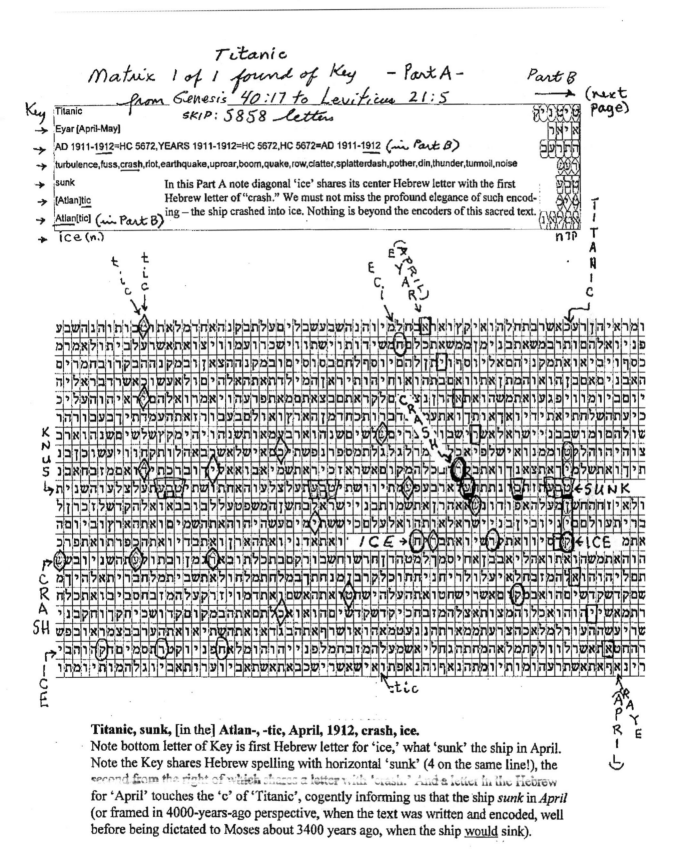

Titanic
Matrix 1 of 1 found of Key — Part A — Part B → (next page)
from Genesis 40:17 to Leviticus 21:5
SKIP: 5858 letters

Titanic, sunk, [in the] Atlan-, -tic, April, 1912, crash, ice.
Note bottom letter of Key is first Hebrew letter for 'ice,' what 'sunk' the ship in April.
Note the Key shares Hebrew spelling with horizontal 'sunk' (4 on the same line!), the
second from the right of which shares a letter with 'crash.' And a letter in the Hebrew
for 'April' touches the 'c' of 'Titanic', cogently informing us that the ship *sunk* in *April*
(or framed in 4000-years-ago perspective, when the text was written and encoded, well
before being dictated to Moses about 3400 years ago, when the ship <u>would</u> sink).

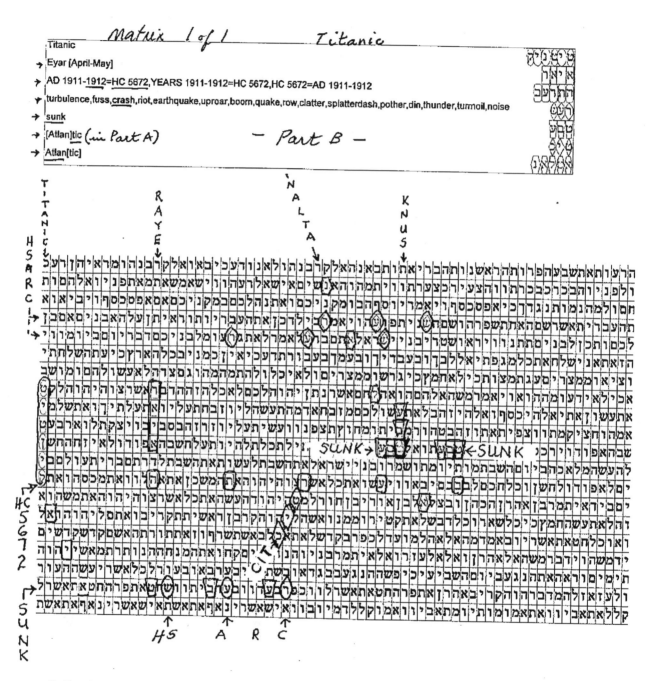

Matrix 1 of 1   *Titanic*

Titanic
- Eyar [April-May]
- AD 1911-1912=HC 5672, YEARS 1911-1912=HC 5672, HC 5672=AD 1911-1912
- turbulence, fuss, crash, riot, earthquake, uproar, boom, quake, row, clatter, splatterdash, pother, din, thunder, turmoil, noise
- sunk
- [Atlan]tic (in Part A)
- Atlan[tic]

— Part B —

In Part B, note horizontal and vertical 'sunk' not only share a Hebrew letter, but also share it with diagonal 'Atlan-.' Note the angle of how 'Atlan-' is spelled (with a skip of 2 letters) recreates, as it intersects with horizontal 'sunk,' the angle of Titanic as it sunk into the Atlantic. The 't' of diagonal '-tic' is only 14 letters to left of diagonal 'Atlan-' (first letter A), and is 12.5% Closer to second letter up the diagonal of 'Atlan-.' Quite a clever stitched-encoding of 'Atlantic,' since the full word was not found encoded.

Part 2 Assassinations

Egypt (Amenemhet, Pharaoh)

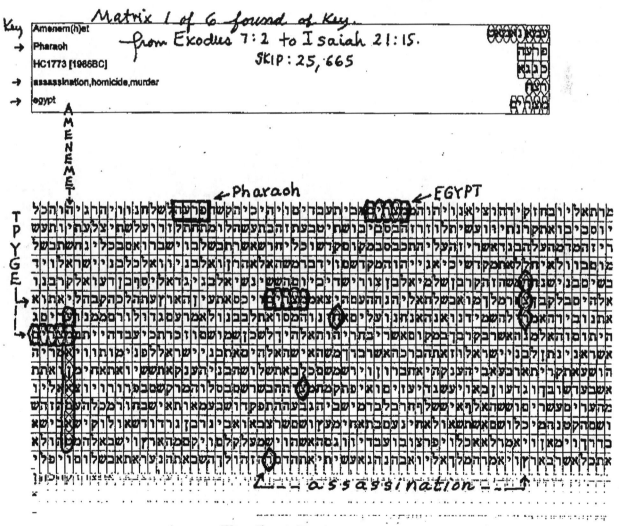

Amenem(h)et, Egypt, Pharaoh, assassination.

Egypt   (An[war] Sadat)

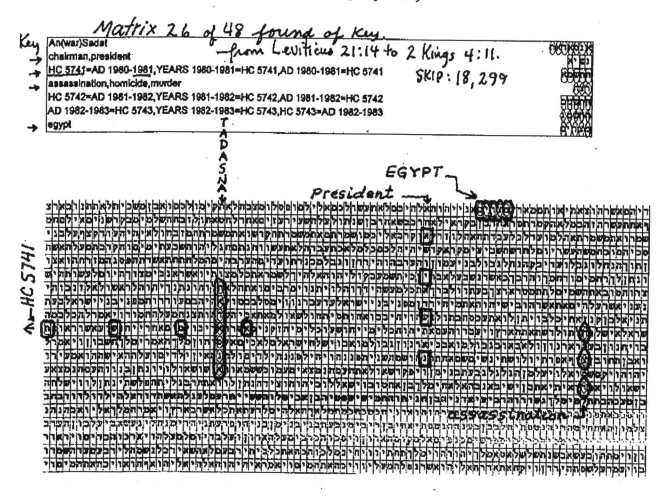

An(war)Sadat, Egypt, president, assassination, HC5741 (1980-1981).

Mahatma Gandhi (also called 'Mohandas' and 'the Mahatma'), was killed on January 30, 1948, by Nathuram Godse. Note correct year is found encoded. The date was not searched for. In full book of *Assassinations* (see Bok List) his other two names are also found encoded, along with his assassin's name.

India   (Mahatma)

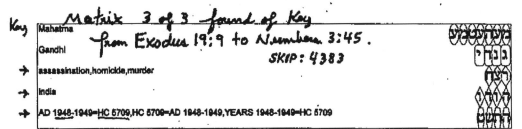

Key

Mahatma	
Gandhi	
→	assassination, homicide, murder
→	India
→	AD 1948-1949=HC 5709, HC 5709=AD 1948-1949, YEARS 1948-1949=HC 5709

Matrix 3 of 3 found of Key from Exodus 19:9 to Numbers 3:45. SKIP: 4383

Mahatma, India, assassination, HC5709 (1948-1949).
This is found in a Torah-only search.
To the right of this screen print are 2 more 'assassination,' and 1 more 'India.'
To left are 2 more 'assassination.'   Matrix #2 has: "Gandhi, assassination,"
from Gen 1:1 to Judges 20:23, skip 24,662 letters.

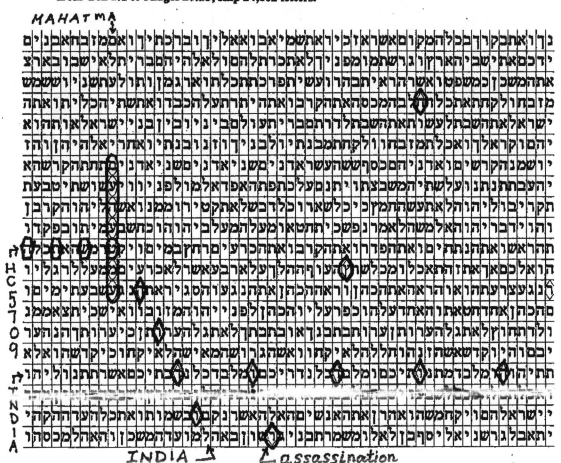

Mexico   (L. Trotsky)

Mexico

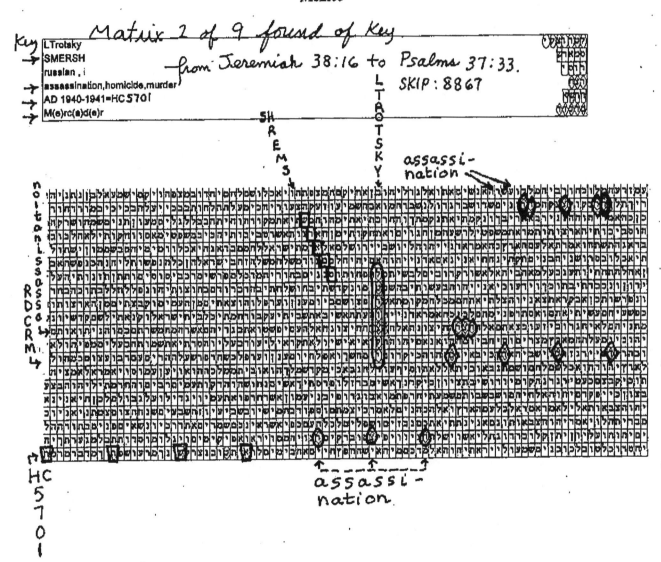

LTrotsky, assassination, HC5701 (1940), [by] Mercader, [of] SMERSH.

'SMERSH' is Russian abbreviation for *smert shpionam* ('Death to Spies'),
Soviet Army counter-espionage organization begun during World War II;
a section of the KGB.

USA (Lincoln)

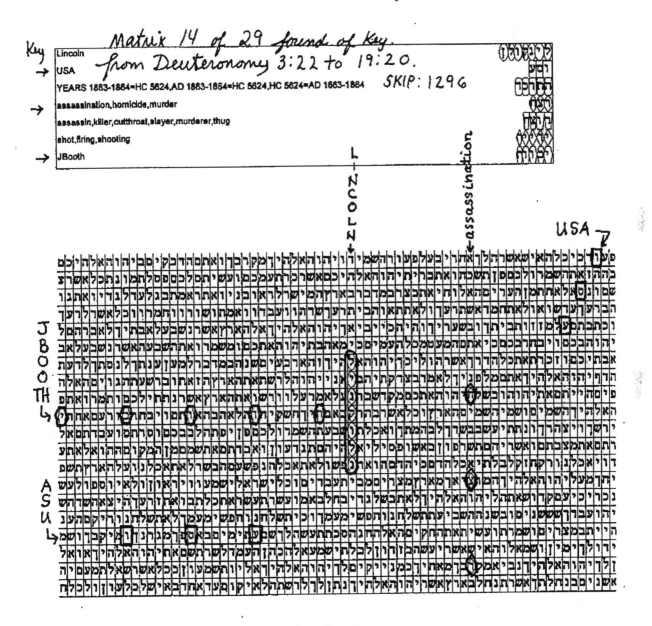

Lincoln, USA, assassination, (by) JBooth.
To right of this screen print are 2 more 'USA,' another 'assassination,' and
another 'Booth,' ... in case we miss the point of the Torah encoders who composed
their text at least 3400 years ago (when it was dictated to Moses by Yahweh).

USA (Kennedy)

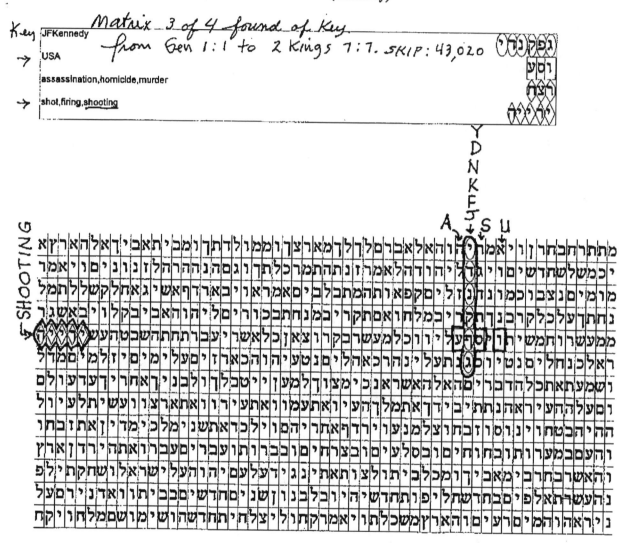

JFK(en)n(e)dy, USA, shooting.
Torah-only search; 4 Keys found.
When all-books are searched for the Key, 67 are found encoded.
When all-books are searched for Key spelled 'J.Kndy', 5760 were found; the
summary of which is: "J.Kndy USA assassination HC5724 (1963), Dallas,
(by) assassin Oswald." The date of November 22 might also be encoded but
was not searched for at this time. Other researches might have found it encoded.

USA   (M.L. King)

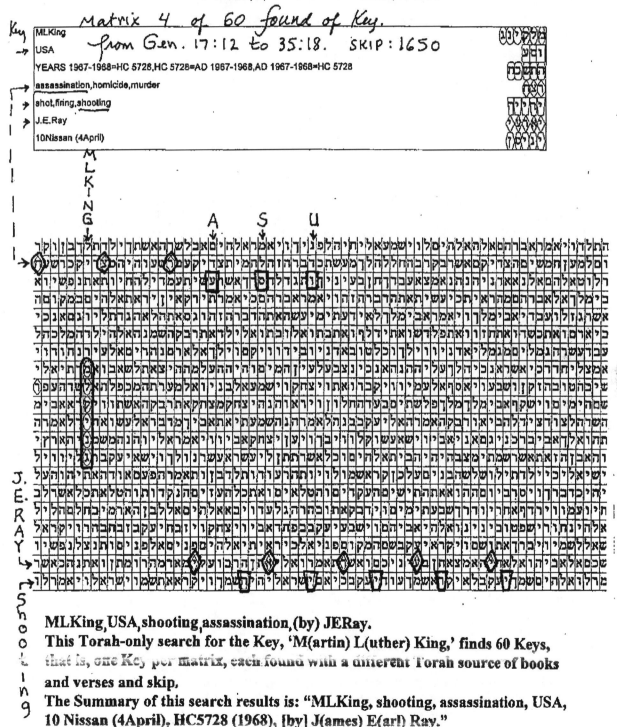

TORAH - ONLY SEARCH

Matrix 4 of 60 found of Key.
from Gen. 17:12 to 35:18.   SKIP: 1650

MLKing, USA, shooting, assassination, (by) JERay.

This Torah-only search for the Key, 'M(artin) L(uther) King,' finds 60 Keys, that is, one Key per matrix, each found with a different Torah source of books and verses and skip.

The Summary of this search results is: "MLKing, shooting, assassination, USA, 10 Nissan (4April), HC5728 (1968), [by] J(ames) E(arl) Ray."

USA   (R.F. Kennedy)

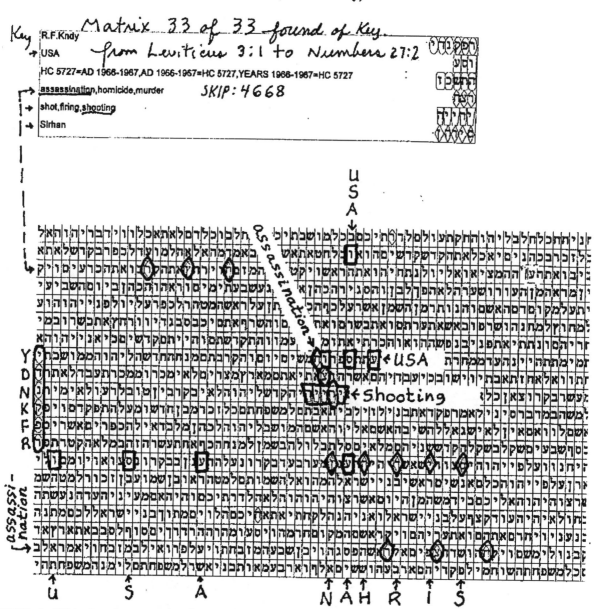

RFKndy USA shooting assassination (by) Sirh(a)n.
Note in the center of this screen print the shared letter of 'assassination' and 'shooting' ...
closely related in concept and execution (so to speak) the Torah encoders entertain us with
another amazing demonstration of their abilities. Note near the end of the horizontal
'Sirh(a)n,' on its left side (in correct Hebrew spelling direction) there is placed a seemingly
random 'A' (of the USA search) found encoded and precisely placed between the 'H' and
'N', exactly where it needs to be for the correct, full spelling, but of course not sequenced
properly for the equidistant spacing called for to qualify as Bible encoding, but neverthe-
less exactly the letter needed to spell his name.

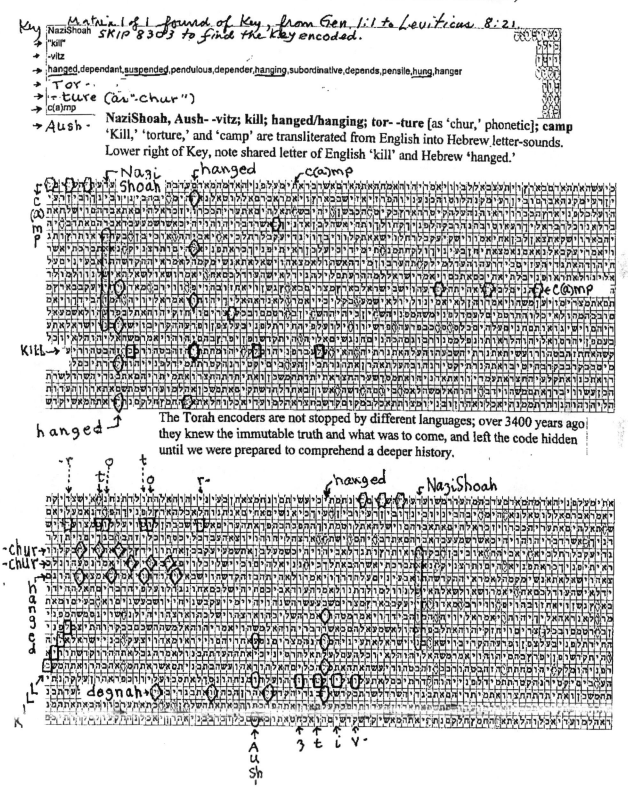

NaziShoah, Aush- -vitz; kill; hanged/hanging; tor- -ture [as 'chur,' phonetic]; **camp**
'Kill,' 'torture,' and 'camp' are transliterated from English into Hebrew letter-sounds.
Lower right of Key, note shared letter of English 'kill' and Hebrew 'hanged.'

The Torah encoders are not stopped by different languages; over 3400 years ago
they knew the immutable truth and what was to come, and left the code hidden
until we were prepared to comprehend a deeper history.

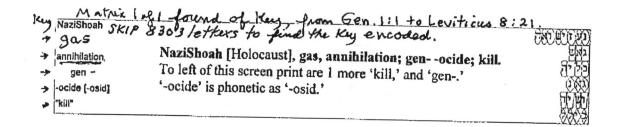

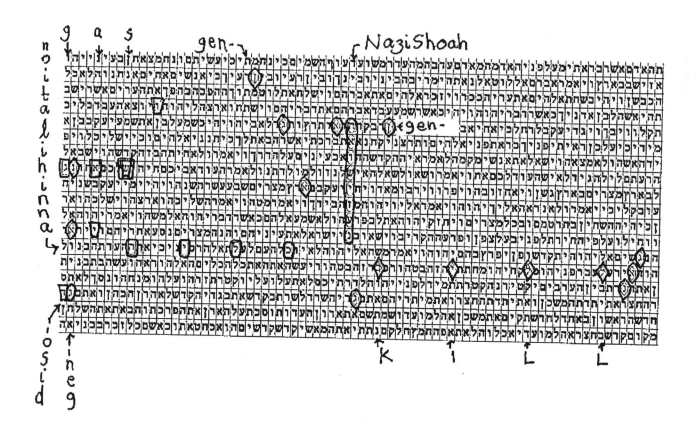

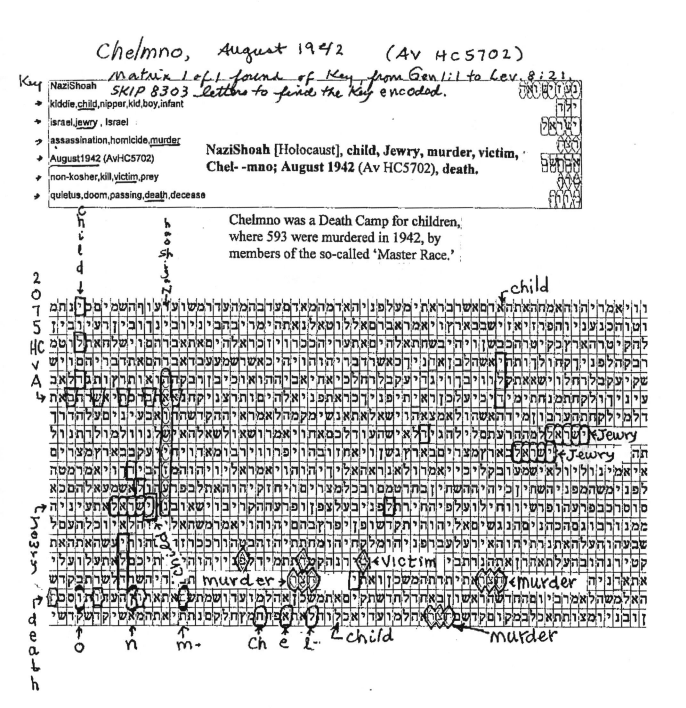

Chelmno, August 1942   (Av HC 5702)

matrix left found of Key, from Gen 1:1 to Lev. 8:21,
SKIP 8303 letters to find the Key encoded.

Key

- NaziShoah
- kiddie, child, nipper, kid, boy, infant
- israel, jewry, Israel
- assassination, homicide, murder
- August1942 (AvHC5702)
- non-kosher, kill, victim, prey
- quietus, doom, passing, death, decease

NaziShoah [Holocaust], child, Jewry, murder, victim,
Chel- -mno; August 1942 (Av HC5702), death.

Chelmno was a Death Camp for children,
where 593 were murdered in 1942, by
members of the so-called 'Master Race.'

To right we see more 'child;' to left are more 'child,' a 'death,' and a 'Jewry.'
'Chel- -mno' is on and near bottom row. The month and year these 593 children
were murdered at this death camp is encoded so it touches and crosses the Key.
Are we getting the message? See 'Proximity' note in the Introduction.

Aurora, Colorado, July 20, 2012.

Twelve shot dead by James Holmes during midnight showing of new Batman movie, "Dark Knight Rises." All names found Torah-encoded, shown in full Report; see Book List and ordering information.

Key

| AuroraCO |
| 1Av (July20) |
| HC5772 (2011-12) |
| shooting, fire |
| dark, |
| knight |
| rose, risen. |

Matrix 1 of 2 found of key.
from Gen 1:1 to Deut. 31:8   skip: 19, 376 letters

AuroraCO, July 20 (1 Av), HC5772 (2011-12), shooting, Dark, Knight, Risen.
The shooting occurred on July 20, 2012. "Rises" wasn't found in Hebrew dictionary, so "risen" was adopted for the Batman movie title.   More parts are encoded left and right of this screen print, and some more could be labeled here. Matrix #2 has all same parts encoded, except year, and is equally dense with encoded elements.

16

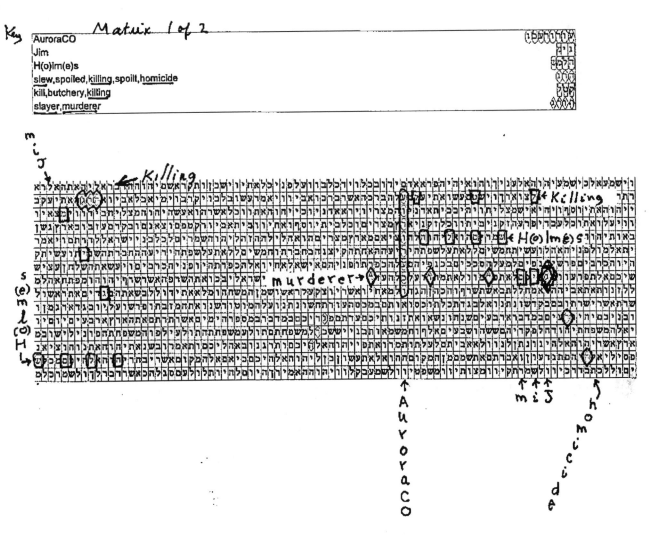

AuroraCO, Jim, H(o)lm(e)s; killing, homicide, murderer.
His first name 'James' found here as 'Jim,' and last name as
phonetic, consistent with Bible Code methodology.
Significantly, 'Jim' is found encoded sharing letter with
Hebrew word for 'murderer' and with 'homicide/killing/slew.'
To right is another 'Jim, homicide' with a shared letter.

Columbine Highschool, Colorado, April 20, 1999.

Thirteen shot dead by Eric Harris and Dylan Kiebold. All names shown in full Report as found Torah-encoded; see Book List for ordering information.

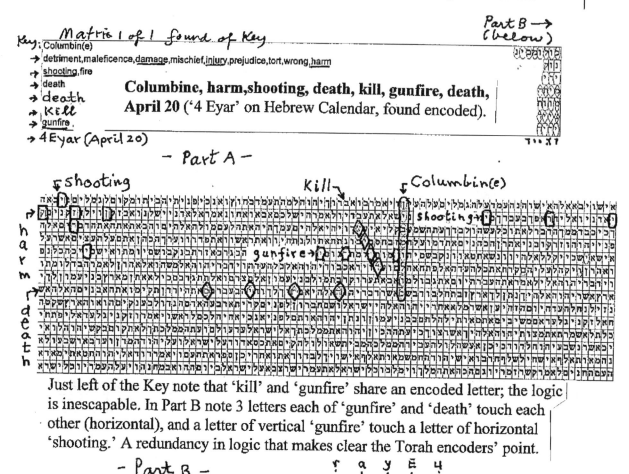

Just left of the Key note that 'kill' and 'gunfire' share an encoded letter; the logic is inescapable. In Part B note 3 letters each of 'gunfire' and 'death' touch each other (horizontal), and a letter of vertical 'gunfire' touch a letter of horizontal 'shooting.' A redundancy in logic that makes clear the Torah encoders' point.

All on April 20 ('4 Eyar' found encoded in Part B), the exact date of this mass murder. All the victims' names and the two shooters are shown encoded in the full Report, available directly from the author via postal mail.

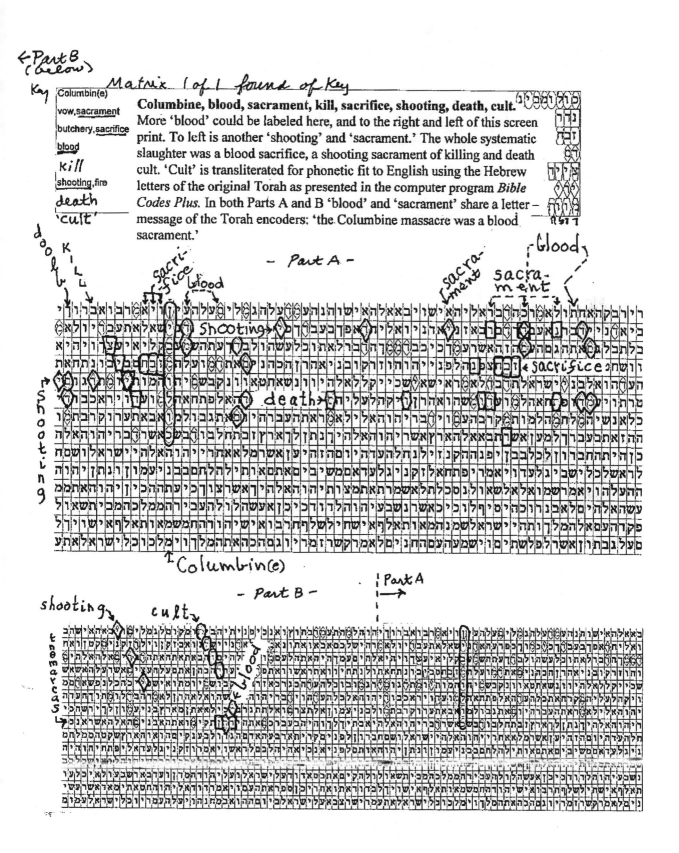

Matrix 1 of 1 found of Key

Columbine, blood, sacrament, kill, sacrifice, shooting, death, cult.
More 'blood' could be labeled here, and to the right and left of this screen print. To left is another 'shooting' and 'sacrament.' The whole systematic slaughter was a blood sacrifice, a shooting sacrament of killing and death cult. 'Cult' is transliterated for phonetic fit to English using the Hebrew letters of the original Torah as presented in the computer program *Bible Codes Plus*. In both Parts A and B 'blood' and 'sacrament' share a letter – message of the Torah encoders: 'the Columbine massacre was a blood sacrament.'

Key
Columbin(e)
vow, sacrament
butchery, sacrifice
blood
kill
shooting, fire
death
'cult'

← Part B
(below)

– Part A –

– Part B –

Part A

Kent State University, Ohio, May 4, 1970.

Four students were shot by National Guard troops. Full Report shows their names found Torah-encoded. See Book List for Ordering information.

Part B →
(below)

Key:
KentSta(te)
civilize, edify, teach, breed, school, rear, train, educate
Ohio
shooting, fire
gunfire
death
arm, weapons, arms

Matrix 1 of 1 found of Key, from Number 26:57 to Deut. 30:4.
SKip 3239 letters to find Key.
odds: 1 in 300.

KentSta(te), school, Ohio, shooting, gunfire, death, weapons.
An interesting phonetic factor here is pronunciation of the Key with or without the last 't' sound has exactly the same effect on the ear as used in conversation. Much of Bible Code research is phonetics-based. More 'shooting' could be labeled here.

— Part A —

gunfire   KentSta(te)

weapons→

←school

Ohio→

Ohio→ ←shooting

— Part B — ┌gunfire   Ohio→   ┌Ohio

←shooting   ←death

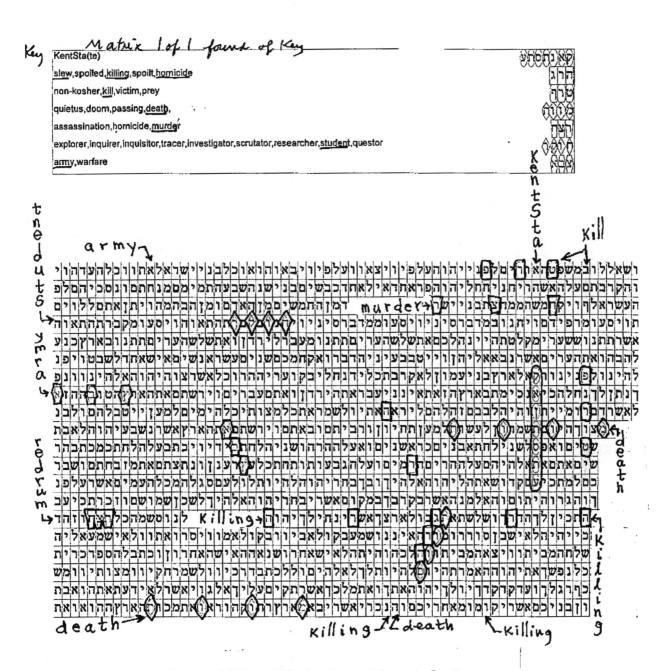

KentSta(te), **killing, kill, death, murder, student, army.**
The National Guard was sent to the campus to control an
anti-Vietnam-war demonstration, and from far away, four
students were shot dead by the army troops (who later were
convicted of conspiracy to commit murder) on May 4, 1970.
In other Matrix print the month and year are shown encoded.

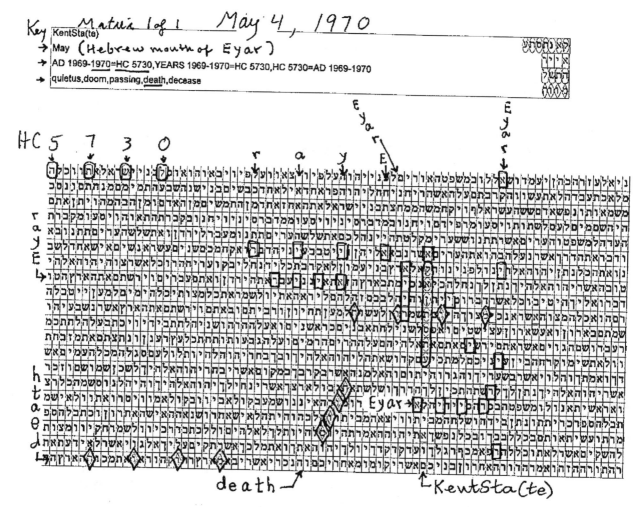

KentSta(te), **Eyar** (May), **HC5730** (AD 1969-70), **death.**
To right nearby is another 'Eyar' and HC5730, very close to each other. While the 4th of May, the day of the shooting, was not found encoded, the month of May was found.

Insofar as the Torah seems to be predictive, having been composed and encoded at least 3500 years ago, and dictated to Moses by YHWH on Mt. Sinai about 3400 years ago (according to Conservative Hebrew tradition), how would have anyone known that long ago what was going to happen so far in the relative future? Or are the Torah encoders in control of that future?

Other factors of this murderous event have already been established as encoded in this one-of-one Torah Matrix, such as 'shooting, school, Ohio, gunfire, weapons, kill, murder, student, army,' so we can visualize them here also found encoded, highlighted, and labeled.

SandyHook Massacre – Where, What, Who, When, How, With What Weapon

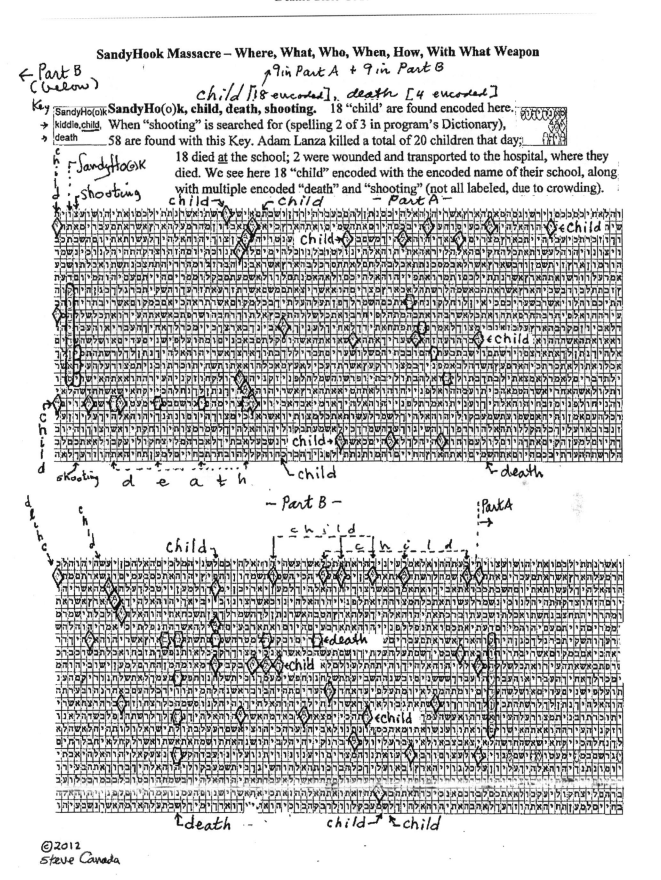

9 in Part A + 9 in Part B

child [18 encoded], death [4 encoded]

Key SandyHo(o)k, child, death, shooting.   18 "child" are found encoded here.
→ kiddle, child, When "shooting" is searched for (spelling 2 of 3 in program's Dictionary),
→ death   58 are found with this Key. Adam Lanza killed a total of 20 children that day;
18 died at the school; 2 were wounded and transported to the hospital, where they
died. We see here 18 "child" encoded with the encoded name of their school, along
with multiple encoded "death" and "shooting" (not all labeled, due to crowding).

– Part A –

– Part B –

Part A →

23

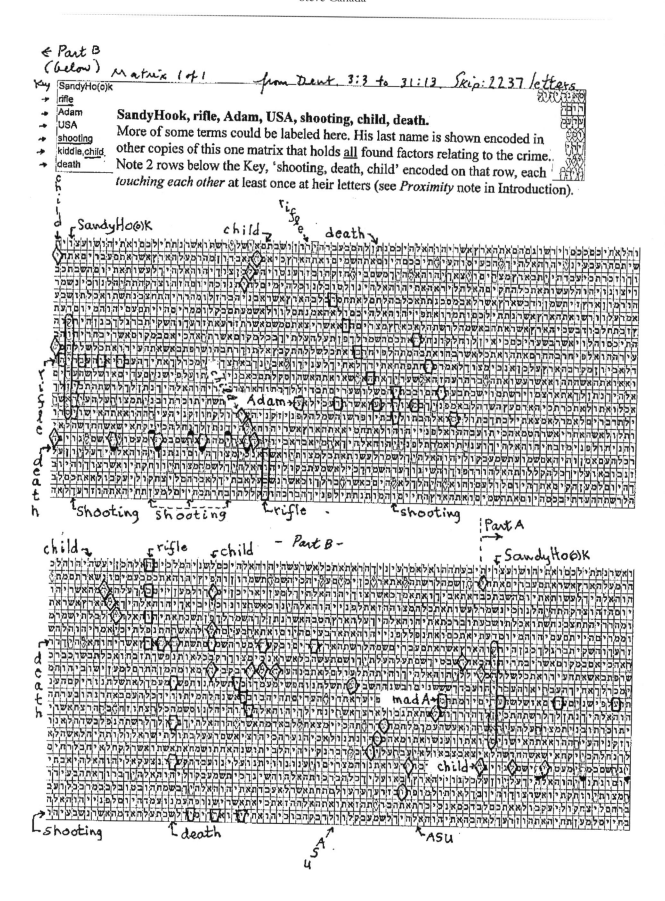

← Part B
(below)   Matrix 1 of 1   from Deut. 3:3 to 31:13. Skip: 2237 letters

Key SandyHo(o)k
→ rifle
→ Adam
→ USA
→ shooting
→ kiddle, child
→ death

SandyHook, rifle, Adam, USA, shooting, child, death.
More of some terms could be labeled here. His last name is shown encoded in
other copies of this one matrix that holds <u>all</u> found factors relating to the crime.
Note 2 rows below the Key, 'shooting, death, child' encoded on that row, each
touching each other at least once at heir letters (see *Proximity* note in Introduction).

Santa Monica, California, June 7, 2013. Five shot dead by gunman.

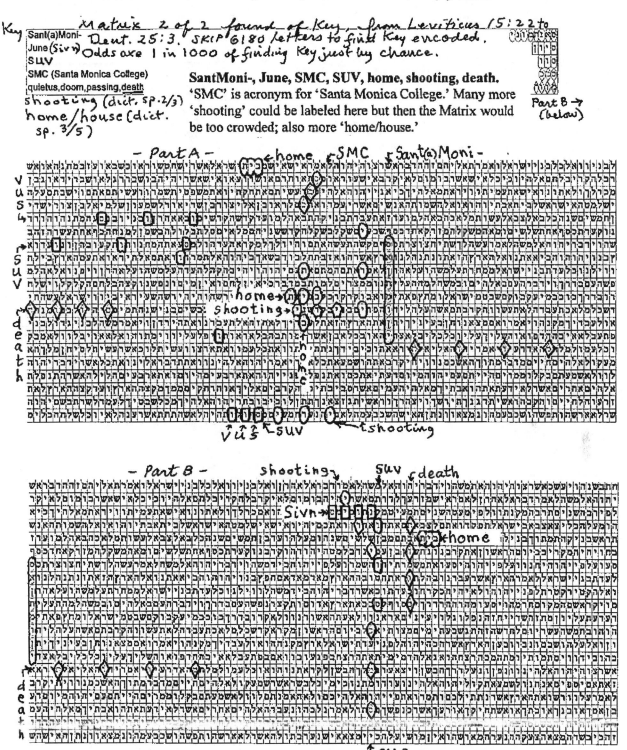

Shooter shot into the family home, which burned, killing two, his father and brother.
He then shot into a red SUV, killing the driver; then on campus, killing more.

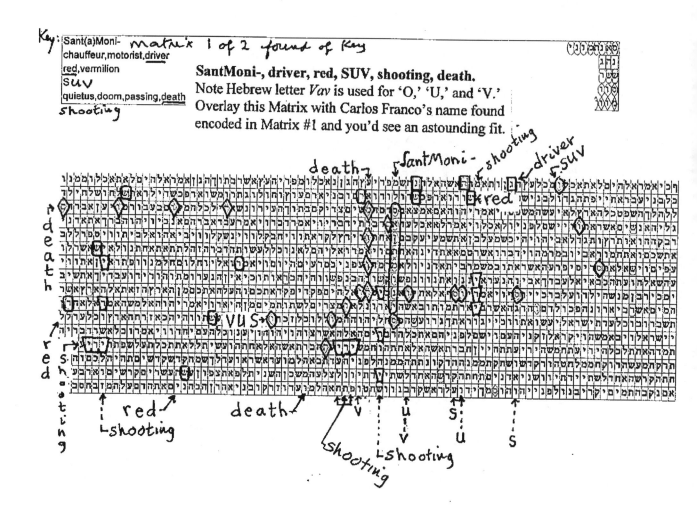

Key: Sant(a)Moni-
chauffeur, motorist, driver
red, vermilion
SUV
quietus, doom, passing, death
shooting

matrix 1 of 2 found of Key

SantMoni-, driver, red, SUV, shooting, death.
Note Hebrew letter *Vav* is used for 'O,' 'U,' and 'V.'
Overlay this Matrix with Carlos Franco's name found
encoded in Matrix #1 and you'd see an astounding fit.

He was the *driver* of the *red SUV* shot to death by the shooter, John Zawahri.
His passenger was his daughter, Marcela Franco, age 26, who died in the
hospital late Saturday night June 8 or on Sunday June 9, having suffered a
serious head wound.
Many more 'shooting' could be labeled here.

In full Report of Mass Shootings, this Santa Monica College event shows all
the names of the shooter and his five victims encoded in either or both of the
two Matrices found of the Key. See Book List for ordering information.

Tucson, Arizona, January 8, 2011.

Six people were shot dead at a political rally for Rep. Gabrielle Giffords, who was wounded. Names of those who died are shown found Torah-encoded in the full Report; see Book List for ordering information.

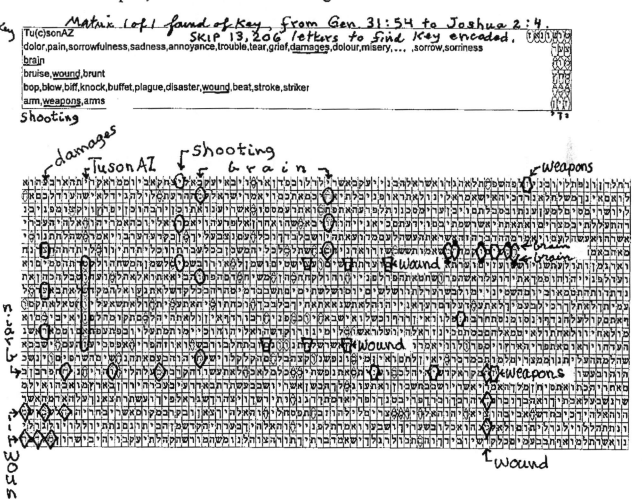

Tu(c)sonAZ, [Rep. Gabrielle Giffords, name found encoded in other print of this Matrix, suffered a] **brain wound damages** [from the], **weapons, shooting.**

More of some could be labeled here, and more are to left of this screen print, including "shot," along with the state's name fully spelled out as encoded.

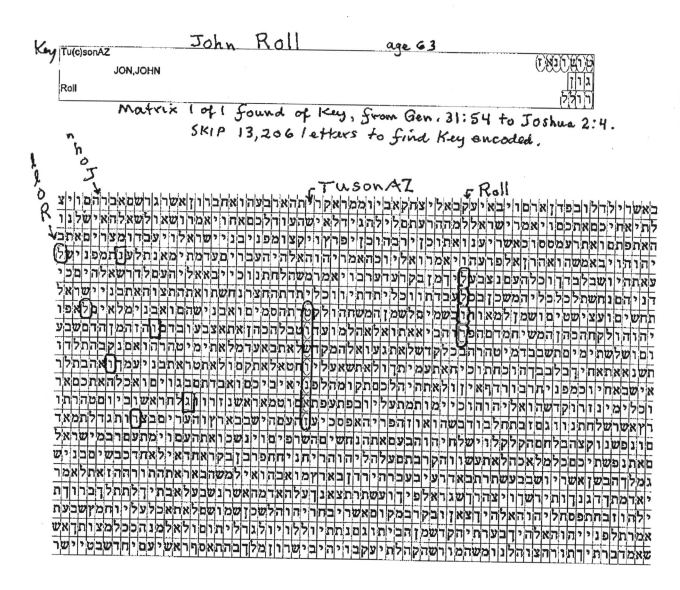

Key Tu(c)sonAZ   John Roll   age 63

JON,JOHN

Roll

Matrix 1 of 1 found of Key, from Gen. 31:54 to Joshua 2:4.
SKIP 13,206 letters to find Key encoded.

TusonAZ, John, Roll.

He was one of the 6 victims who died. He was age 63. Other factors of the
mass shooting (including the shooter's name) such as 'shooting, weapons,
shot, death,' are in prior matrices (all shown in the full Report available
directly from the author) with the Key, so don't need to be labeled here again.

Part 5 Natural Disasters

Earthquakes: 'Temblors'

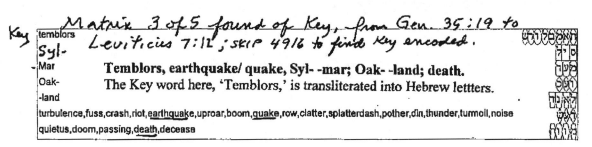

Matrix 3 of 5 found of Key, from Gen. 35:19 to Leviticus 7:12; skip 4916 to find Key encoded.

Temblors, earthquake/ quake, Syl- -mar; Oak- -land; death.
The Key word here, 'Temblors,' is transliterated into Hebrew lettters.

turbulence,fuss,crash,riot,earthquake,uproar,boom,quake,row,clatter,splatterdash,pother,din,thunder,turmoil,noise
quietus,doom,passing,death,decease

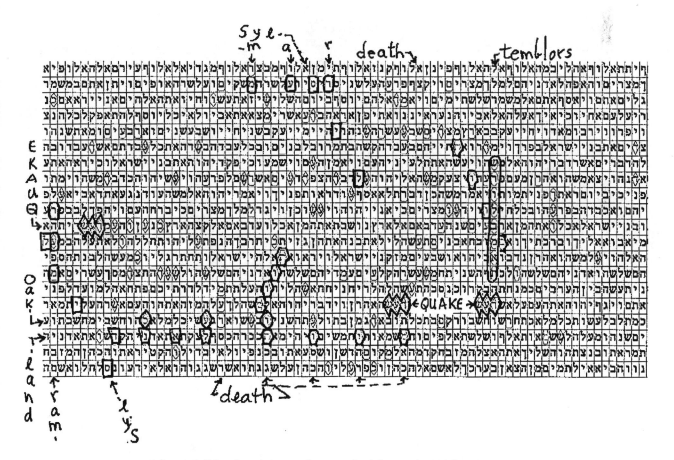

Years of these California quakes to be searched for, and 'California' itself.
It is extra significant that 'death' (spelling 2 of 2 in program's Dictionary)
touches and crosses the Key. More could be labeled here, and more are
to right of this screen print.

2 California Fault Lines: San Andreas, and Hayward

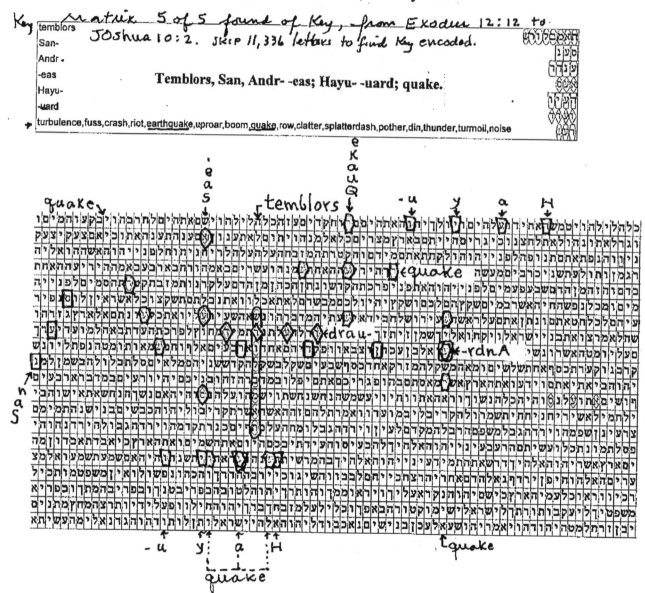

Some more parts are to right. "Cal-ifor-nia" is found in Matcix #2 and #3 with this Key. Note 2 shared 'a' of 'quake', one with 'Andr-' and one with 'Hayu-.' Don't try such encoding of a large text at home, you'll hurt yourself.

2 U.S. Quake Fault Lines: New Madrid, and Kentucky.

Key *Matrix 4 of 5 found of Key, from Leviticus 6:15 to Numbers 5:17; SKIP 2387 letters to find Key encoded.*

Key	temblors
	New
	Mad-
	-rid
	Kent-
	-ucky
	USA

Temblors, New, Mad- -rid; Kent- -ucky; USA, quake, death.
We've seen elsewhere the many 'quake' encoded with this Key.
To left are more parts encoded, except 'Kent-', 'ucky,' and 'USA.'

Fukushima, Japan

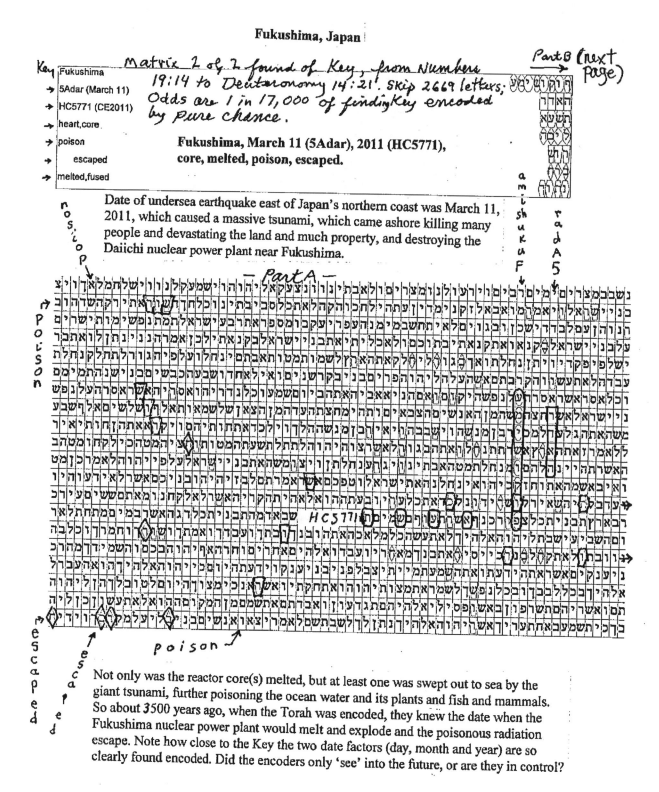

Key Fukushima

→ 5Adar (March 11)
→ HC5771 (CE2011)
→ heart,core
→ poison
→ escaped
→ melted,fused

Matrix 2 of 2 found of Key, from Numbers 19:14 to Deuteronomy 14:21. Skip 2669 letters; Odds are 1 in 17,000 of finding Key encoded by pure chance.

Part B (next page) →

Fukushima, March 11 (5Adar), 2011 (HC5771), core, melted, poison, escaped.

Date of undersea earthquake east of Japan's northern coast was March 11, 2011, which caused a massive tsunami, which came ashore killing many people and devastating the land and much property, and destroying the Daiichi nuclear power plant near Fukushima.

— Part A —

Not only was the reactor core(s) melted, but at least one was swept out to sea by the giant tsunami, further poisoning the ocean water and its plants and fish and mammals. So about *3500* years ago, when the Torah was encoded, they knew the date when the Fukushima nuclear power plant would melt and explode and the poisonous radiation escape. Note how close to the Key the two date factors (day, month and year) are so clearly found encoded. Did the encoders only 'see' into the future, or are they in control?

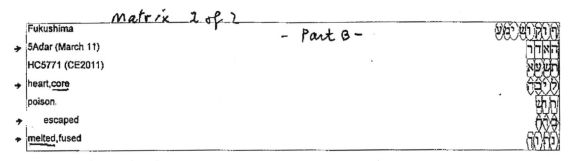

In this Part B, perhaps it is NO accident that the only 2 'core' are encoded so close to 3 'escape,' the vertical, no-skip one even practically *touching* the horizontal 'core' (spelled-encoded in the correct Hebrew reading-writing direction, from right to left).

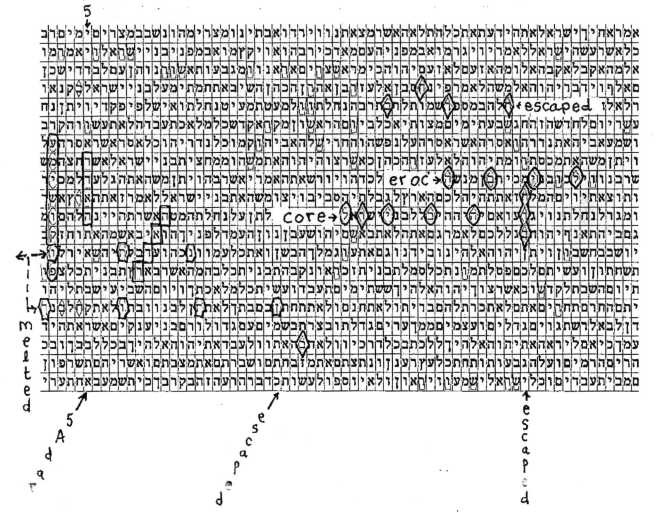

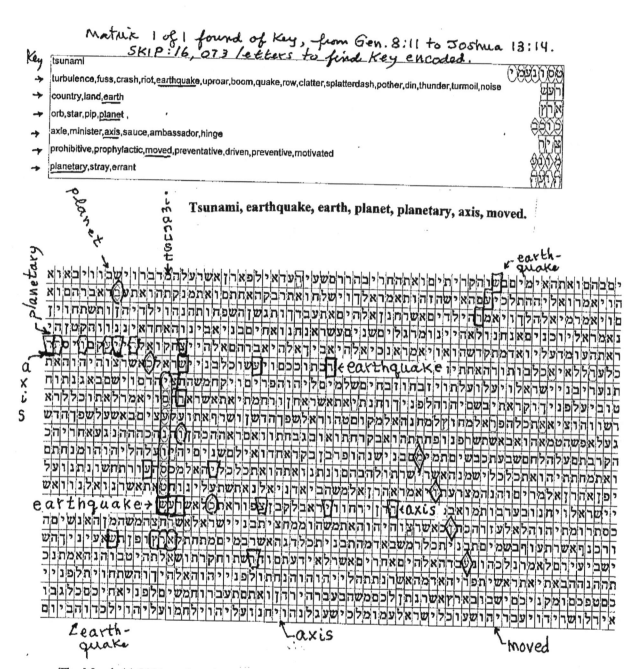

Matrix 1 of 1 found of Key, from Gen. 8:11 to Joshua 13:14.
SKIP: 16,073 letters to find Key encoded.

Key

tsunami

→ turbulence,fuss,crash,riot,earthquake,uproar,boom,quake,row,clatter,splatterdash,pother,din,thunder,turmoil,noise

→ country,land,earth

→ orb,star,pip,planet

→ axle,minister,axis,sauce,ambassador,hinge

→ prohibitive,prophylactic,moved,preventative,driven,preventive,motivated

→ planetary,stray,errant

Tsunami, earthquake, earth, planet, planetary, axis, moved.

The March 11,2011 earthquake and resulting tsunami shifted the Earth's axis between 10 cm (2.54 inches) to 25 cm (10 inches). Will this eventually affect the planet's 'precession'?

Many more aspects of the events are shown found Torah-encoded in the full Report; 106 pages long, including 14 names of the many who died. Only these 14 names were available at the time, that is, found online. See Book List for ordering information.

Hurricanes

Matrix 1 of 3 found of Key, from Gen. 1:24 to Deut. 12:16.
SKIP 13,601 letters to find Key encoded.

Hurrican(e), Flor--rida; Miami, Keys, 1919 (HC5680).
'HC' means 'Hebrew Calendar Year'. 'Keys' here is phonetic transliteration, with 's' as actual 'z' sound using the Hebrew letter *Zayin*.

The 1919 hurricane pounded the Florida Keys and south Texas; 600 killed. It might have affected Miami too, found encoded left of the Key 176 columns.

Part B (below)

Key:
hurrican(e)
FLOR-
-rida
Miami
ton,tone,key
"Keys"
HC 5680=AD 1919-1920

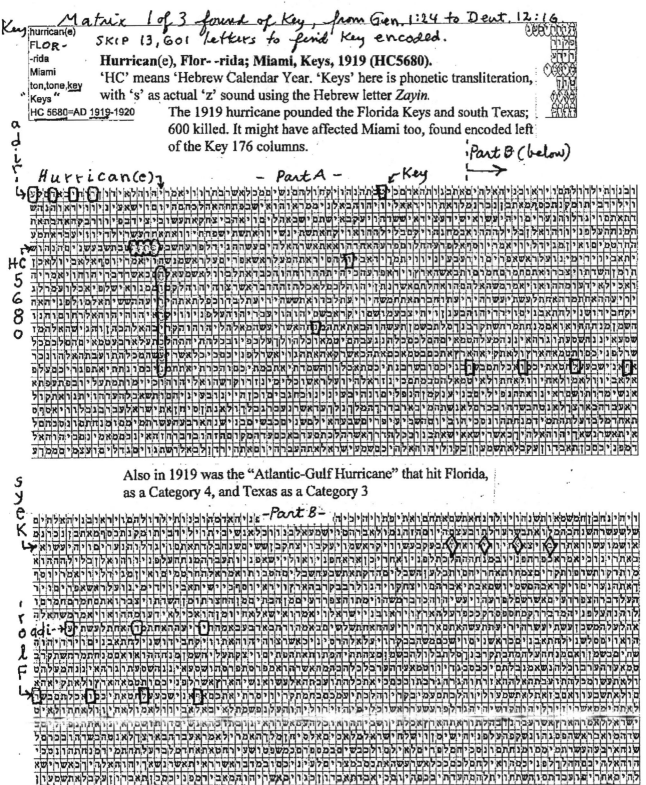

Also in 1919 was the "Atlantic-Gulf Hurricane" that hit Florida, as a Category 4, and Texas as a Category 3

Matrix 1 of 3 found of Key, from Gen 1:24 to Deut. 12:16. SKIP 13,601 letters to find Key encoded.

Hurricane, Flor--rida; Caro--lina; New York.

Three states with many of the U.S. hurricanes. No doubt further searches would reveal the storm names and dates encoded with these storms that have ravaged parts of these states, perhaps even the names of the cities.

Key
hurrican(e)
FLOR-
-rida
Caro-
-lina
New
York

← Part B (below)

— Part A —

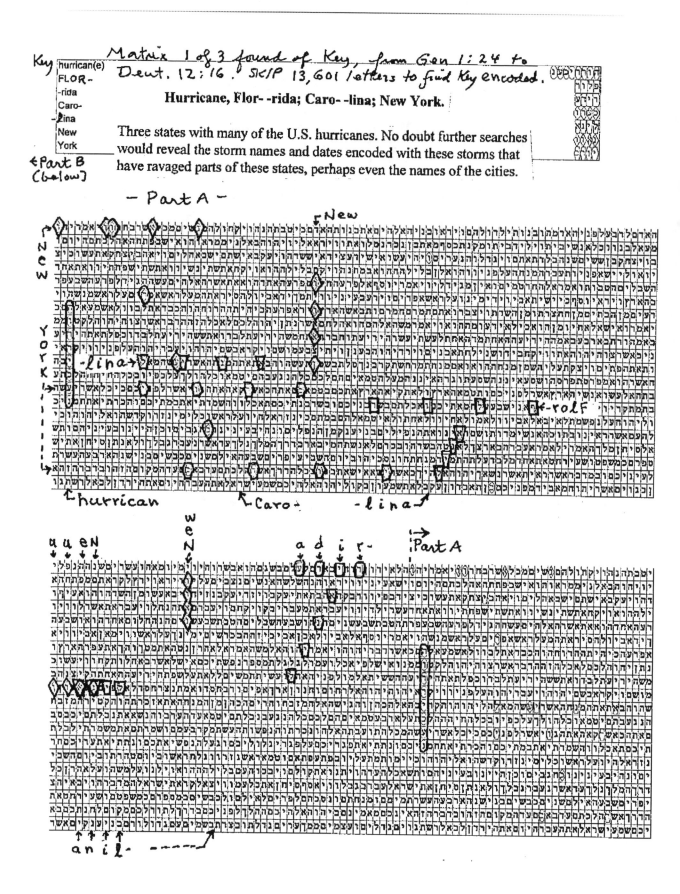

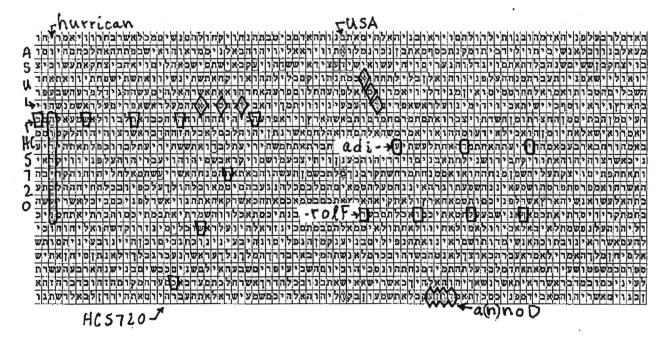

Matrix 1 of 3 found of Key, from Gen 1:24 to Deut. 12:16. SKIP 13601 letters to find Key encoded.

Key
hurrican(e)
FLOR
(ore,know-how,science,ken,knowledge,knew)-ida
Don(n)a
HC 5720=AD 1959-1960.
USA

Florida Hurricane "Donna," 1960.

Hurricane, Flor- -ida; Don(n)a, 1960 (HC5720), USA.

While 'ida' means something in Hebrew (see legend above), it is the phonetic of transliterated sounds this is important in Bible Code research.

Some more parts are to the left of this screen print. Perhaps not so surprisingly, given the amazing encoding capabilities of the Torah composers, note the right-to left encoded spelling of 'Flor- -ida,' and of 'Don(n)a,' which is the correct spelling direction in Hebrew.

5 more -'ida' could be labeled here, and 7 more to left of this screen print.

Tornado

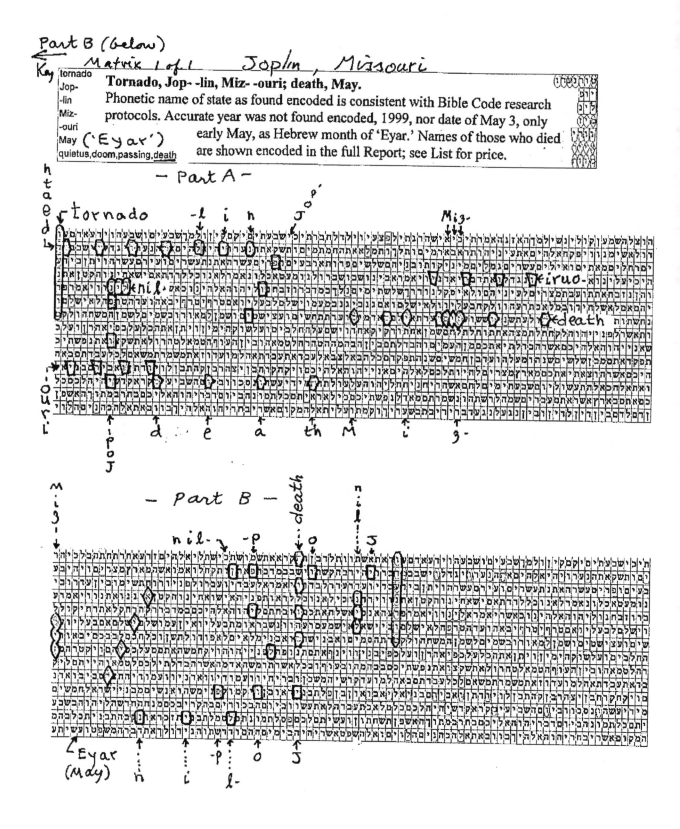

Tornado, Jop- -lin, Miz- -ouri; death, May.
Phonetic name of state as found encoded is consistent with Bible Code research protocols. Accurate year was not found encoded, 1999, nor date of May 3, only early May, as Hebrew month of 'Eyar.' Names of those who died are shown encoded in the full Report; see List for price.

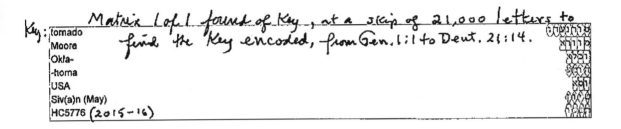

Key:
tornado
Moore
Okla-
-homa
USA
Siv(a)n (May)
HC5776 (2015-16)

Matrix 1 of 1 found of Key, at a skip of 21,000 letters to find the Key encoded, from Gen. 1:1 to Deut. 21:14.

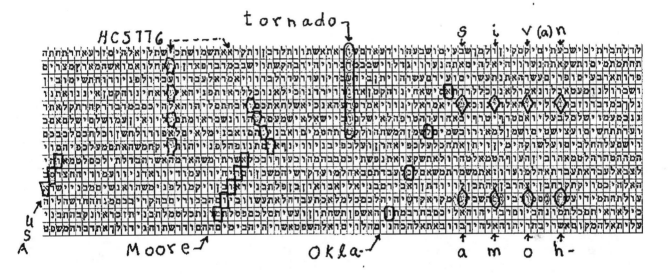

Tornado, Moore, Okla- -homa; USA, Siv(a)n [May], HC5776 (2015-16).
In Hebrew month of May (Sivan), Hebrew Calendar (HC) year 5776 (AD 2015-16).
While the date for the devastating tornado was May 20, 2013, the Gregorian
Calendar we use is between 3 and 9 years too low in its count since the birth of
Jesus of Nazareth (Yeshua), so a finding of encoded year 2015-16 conforms to
what to expect if we account for the calendar adjustment.
Encoded names of the 24 dead on May 20, 2013 are shown in the full Report,
available directly from the author; see Report and Book List for price and
ordering information.

Tornados occur worldwide, in many countries. The country with the
most tornados relative to its size is Britain. The earliest recorded
tornado was in 1091 there, one that knocked down London Bridge.

Tsunami

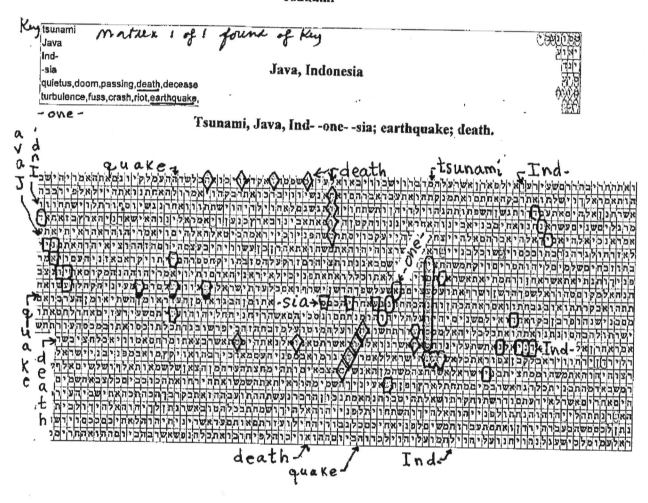

Tsunami, Java, Ind- -one- -sia; earthquake; death.

July 17, 2006 quake (7.7) off SW coast of Java, killed over 300, generated a tsunami.
December 26, 2004, quake (9.3) off coast of Sumatra, created a tsunami that killed
more than 200,000 across several Indian Ocean countries, including Indonesia.
See next Matrix for dates.

Tsunami, Alaska, earthquake, April 1, 1946, USA.

Key tsunami ALA- -ska USA Adar HC 5706 (AD 1945-46) earthquake

Matrix 1 of 1 found of Key, from Gen. 8:11 to Joshua 13:14. SKIP 16,073 letters to find Key encoded.

Tsunami, Ala- -ska; earthquake, Adar, HC5706 (1946), USA.
'Adar' is Hebrew month Feb-March that in 1946 included April 1.
Waves traveled at 600 MPH, and were up to 150-feet high.

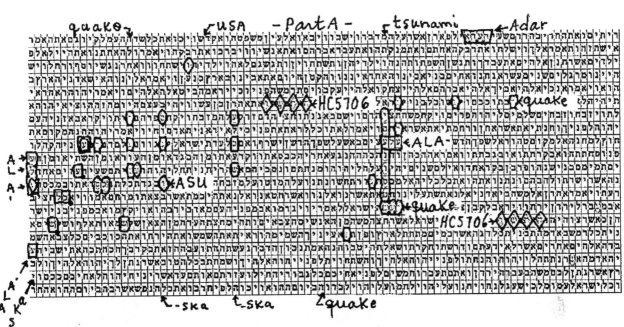

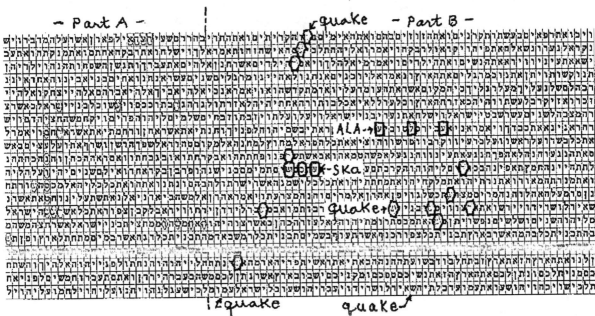

Volcanos:

Krakatoa, Dutch East Indies, 1883.

Key Matrix 1 of 1 found of Key when searched for at its
skip of 7034 letters; from Gen.1:1 to Exodus 36:33.

volcanos
Krak-
-atoa
HC 5640=AD 1879-1880
[report] "Du(t)ch"
east
'Ind(i)e(s)'

Volcanos, Krak- -atoa; Du(t)ch, East, Ind(i)e(s), HC5640.

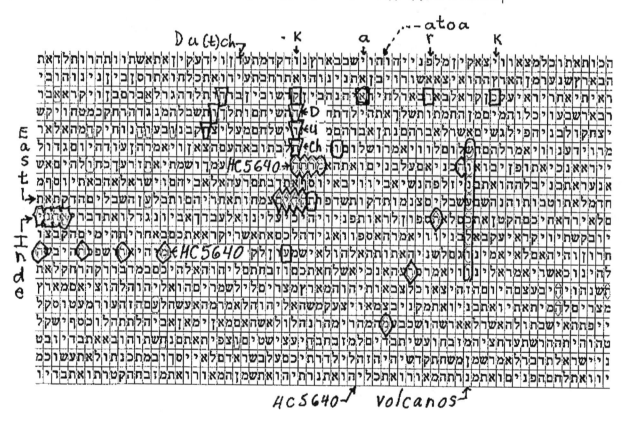

HC5640 volcanos

More could be labeled here, and to right of this screen print.
This volcano erupted on May 20, 1883 through August 26-27, generating a massive tsunami and killing at least 36,417 people. It created the loudest sound ever heard on Earth. The smoke and ash created worldwide cooling of about 1.6 F degrees, for 2 years. HC5640 (1879-80) is about 36 months "off" the actual event, and thus within the needed correction range of the Gregorian Calendar.

Volcanos, (Mount Saint) **Helens, Washington State, USA, 1980.**

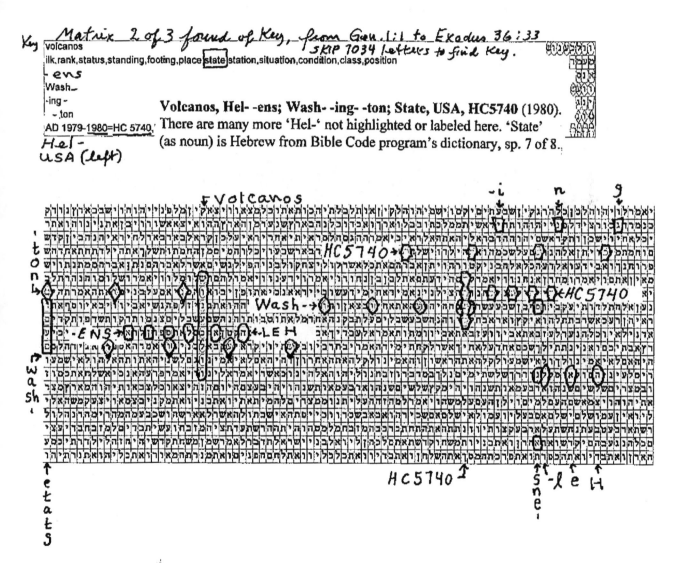

Volcanos, Hel- -ens; Wash- -ing- -ton; State, USA, HC5740 (1980). There are many more 'Hel-' not highlighted or labeled here. 'State' (as noun) is Hebrew from Bible Code program's dictionary, sp. 7 of 8.

Another '-ing-' is 28 columns to left of this screen print. 'USA' is 19 columns to left. While 'ens' means something in Hebrew, we take only the phonetic, to form the sound searched for when transliterated like that.

Volcanos: Pinatubo, Philippines, 1991.

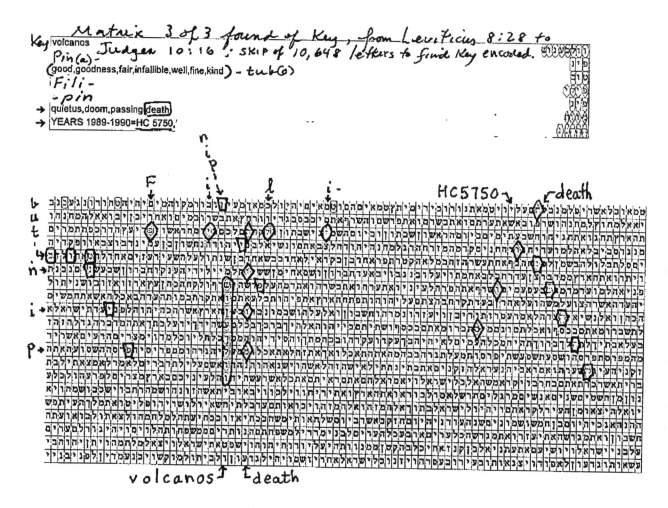

Volcanos, Pin(a)- -tub(o); Fili- -pin(es); death, HC5750 (1990).
More of some parts are to left of this screen print.

'Luzon Island' was not searched for. Hundreds were killed. Year is "off" by only some months; not bad for apparently trying to predict such a natural disaster about 3500 years in the future.
Climate effects were of worldwide cooling because of ash spewed and spread into the atmosphere and carried by trade-winds, blocking some of the sunlight. The author recalls alterations in sunset colors for months as seen from the coast of California.

Part 6   Terror Attacks

Benghazi

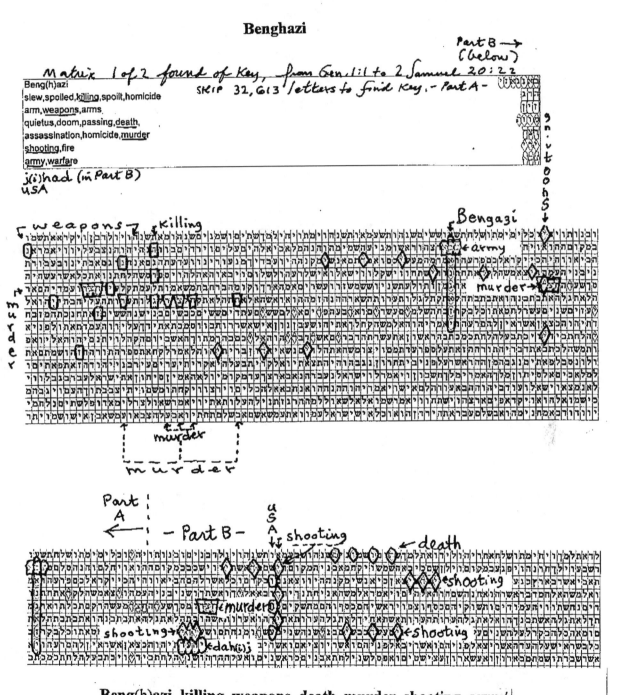

Matrix 1 of 2 found of Key, from Gen. 1:1 to 2 Samuel 20:22
SKIP 32,613 letters to find Key. - Part A -

Part B →
(below)

Beng(h)azi
slew,spolled,killing,spoilt,homicide
arm,weapons,arms
quietus,doom,passing,death,
assassination,homicide,murder
shooting,fire
army,warfare

j(i)had (in Part B)
USA

Beng(h)azi, killing, weapons, death, murder, shooting, army/
warfare, j(i)had, USA.

More 'shooting' could be labeled here; 3 highlighted in Part A
and not labeled. This Matrix 1 of 2 also has 'consulate' encoded
in it (shown in Report with names of victims).

45

← Part B
(below)

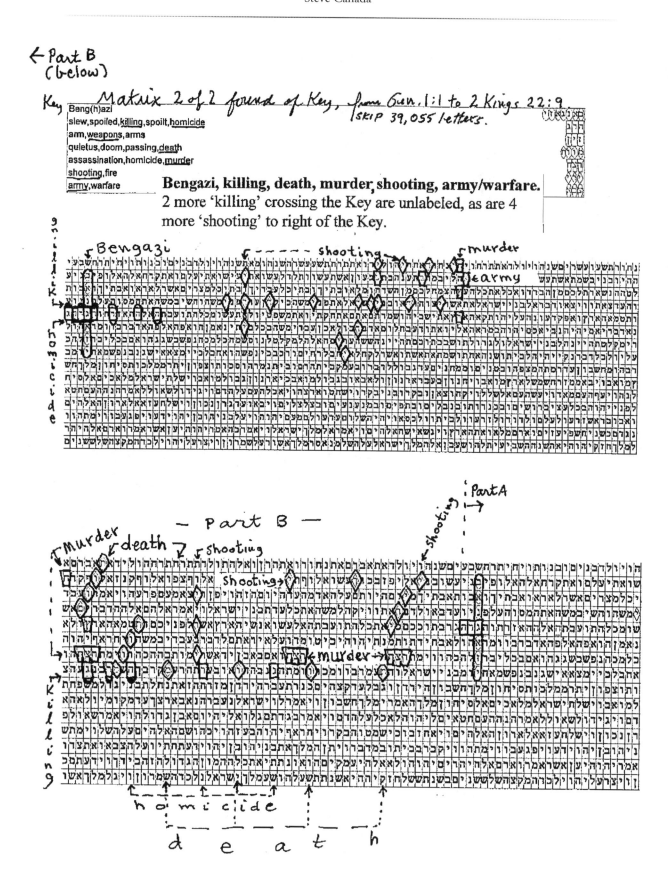

Key

Bang(h)azi
slew, spoiled, killing, spoilt, homicide
arm, weapons, arms
quietus, doom, passing, death
assassination, homicide, murder
shooting, fire
army, warfare

Matrix 2 of 2 found of Key, from Gen. 1:1 to 2 Kings 22:9
SKIP 39,055 letters.

Bengazi, killing, death, murder, shooting, army/warfare.
2 more 'killing' crossing the Key are unlabeled, as are 4
more 'shooting' to right of the Key.

Boston Marathon Bombing

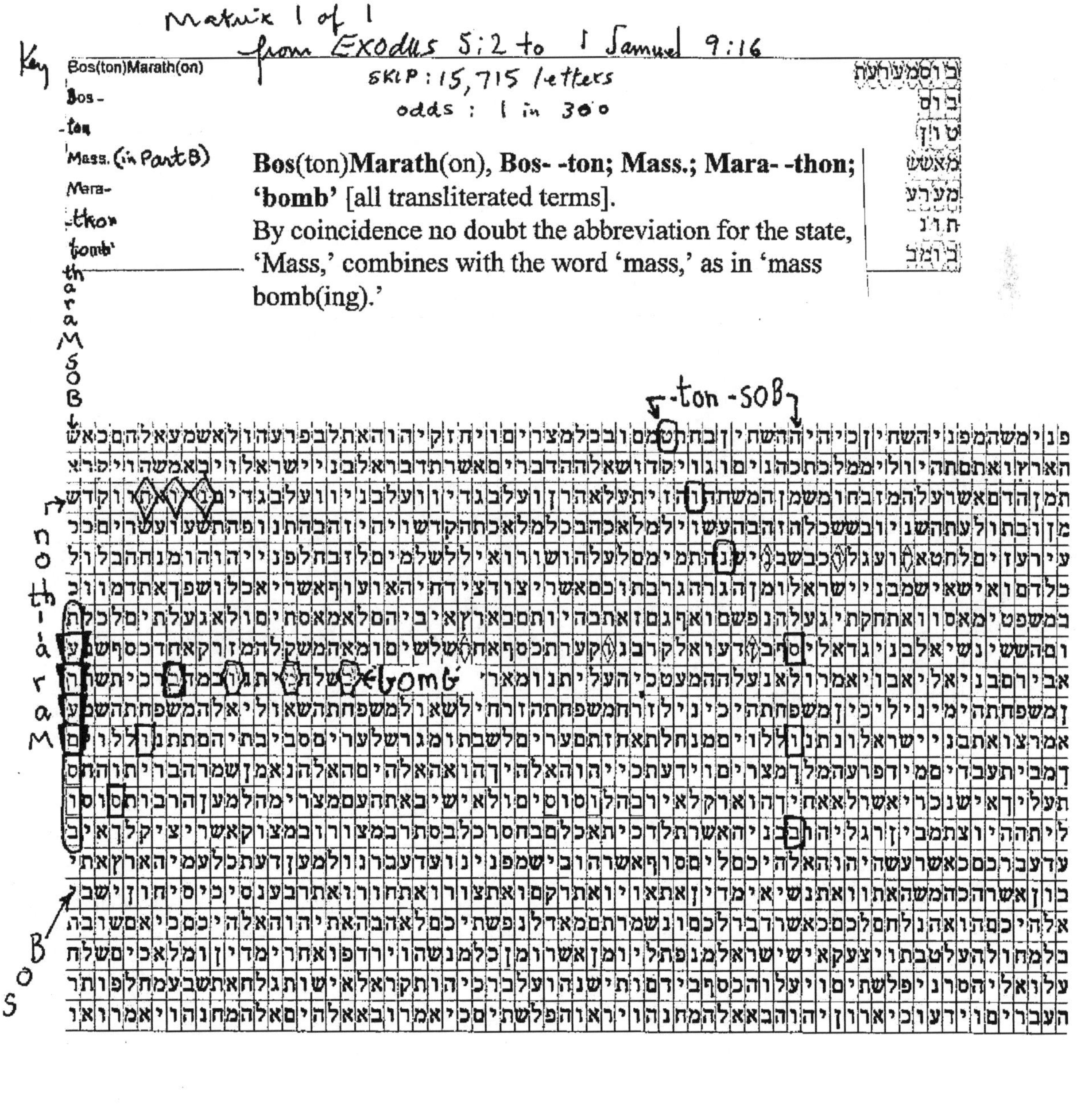

Matrix 1 of 1
from Exodus 5:2 to 1 Samuel 9:16
SKIP: 15,715 letters
odds: 1 in 300

Key
Bos(ton)Marath(on)
Bos-
-ton
Mass. (in Part B)
Mara-
-thon
bomb
th
a
r
a
M
S
O
B

Bos(ton)Marath(on), Bos- -ton; Mass.; Mara- -thon; 'bomb' [all transliterated terms].
By coincidence no doubt the abbreviation for the state, 'Mass,' combines with the word 'mass,' as in 'mass bomb(ing).'

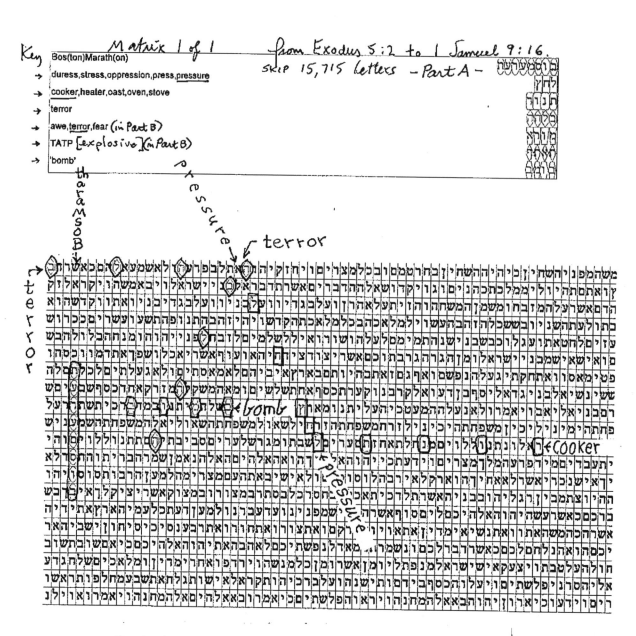

**Bos(ton)Marath(on), pressure, cooker, bomb, terror,
TATP [an explosive], terror.**

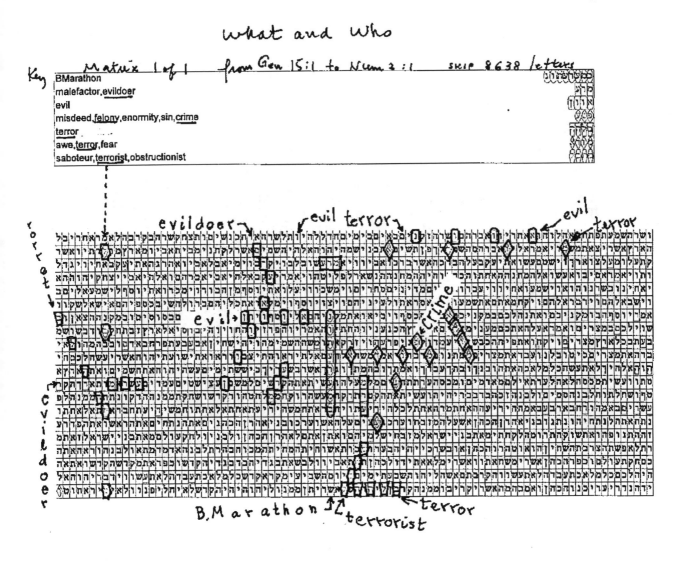

Bmarathon, evildoer, evil, crime, terror, terrorist.
More of some parts are to left and right of this screen print.

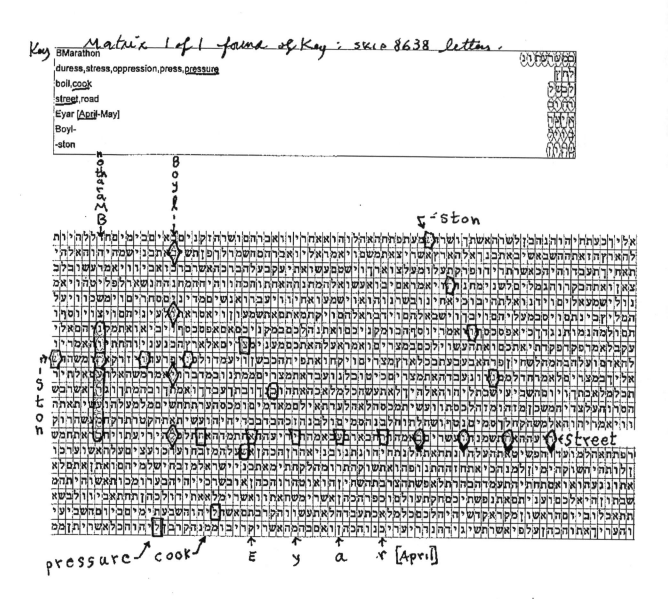

Bmarathon, pressure, cook, April (Eyar), Boyl- -ston; street.
To left of this screen print are 2 more 'cook,' 2 more 'Boyl-,'
and 1 more 'Eyar' (April), all close to each other.
All victims names are found encoded, using both versions of
the Key, presented in the full Report. Also the full spelling of
the two Chechen terrorists' names, along with 'Why' — 'Islam,
terror, fervor, jihad, hate, USA.'

Fort Hood

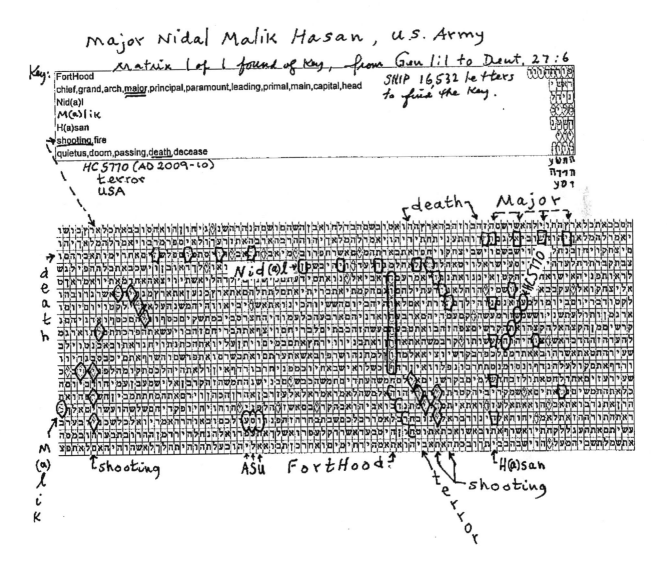

major Nidal Malik Hasan, U.S. Army
matrix 1 of 1 found of Key, from Gen 1:1 to Deut. 27:6
SHIP 16,532 letters to find the Key.

FortHood, Major, Nid(a)l, M(a)lik, H(a)san, shooting, death, terror, USA, HC5770 (AD 2009-10).

More 'shooting' could be labeled here and to the right and left of this screen print. In other prints in the full Report, the town is found encoded, as is 'TX,' and all the names of his victims, along with 'army'

51

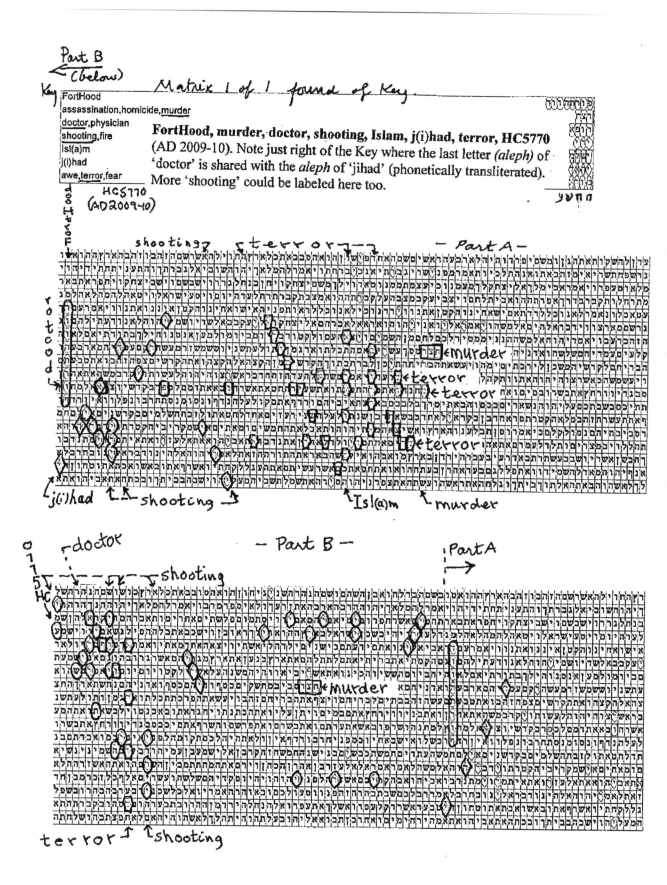

Part B
(below)

Matrix 1 of 1 found of Key.

Key

FortHood
assassination,homicide,murder
doctor,physician
shooting,fire
Isl(a)m
j(i)had
awe,terror,fear

FortHood, murder, doctor, shooting, Islam, j(i)had, terror, HC5770
(AD 2009-10). Note just right of the Key where the last letter *(aleph)* of
'doctor' is shared with the *aleph* of 'jihad' (phonetically transliterated).
More 'shooting' could be labeled here too.

HC5770
(AD2009-10)

— Part A —
shooting   ← terror →

j(i)had ← shooting →   Isl(a)m   murder

doctor   — Part B —   Part A

shooting

murder

terror   shooting

9/11: Twin Tower, New York City

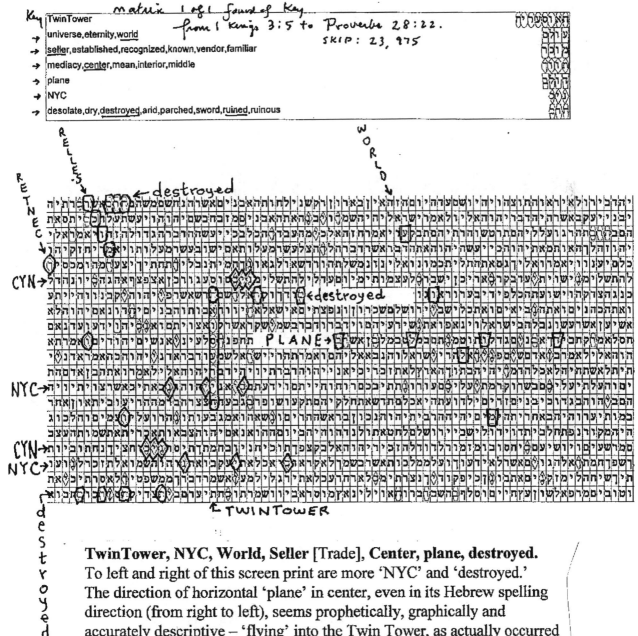

TwinTower, NYC, World, Seller [Trade], Center, plane, destroyed.
To left and right of this screen print are more 'NYC' and 'destroyed.'
The direction of horizontal 'plane' in center, even in its Hebrew spelling
direction (from right to left), seems prophetically, graphically and
accurately descriptive – 'flying' into the Twin Tower, as actually occurred
on that crisp September morning of the 11th, in 2001.
Note the last letter of one of the many 'destroyed' is the first letter of the
vertical Key, 'Twin Tower.'

9/11

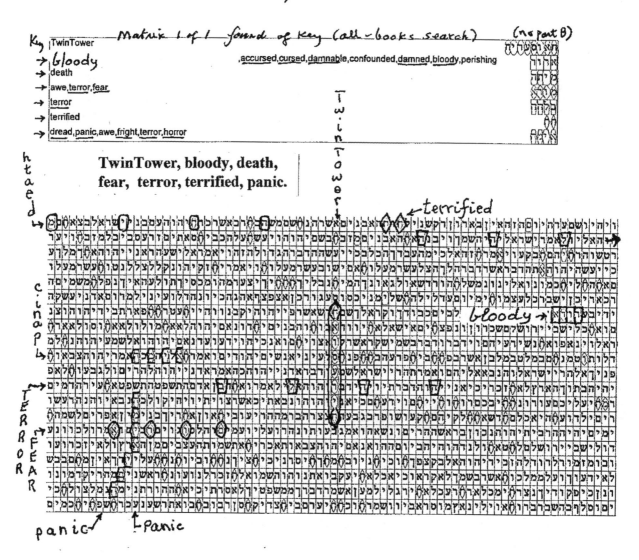

**TwinTower, bloody, death,
fear, terror, terrified, panic.**

Note the Key begins and ends with the 2 letters of 'terrified,' as if destiny itself
was written into the building's architectural demise, as the occupants became
terrified from the attack.

The 2 'panic' in lower left, joined and sharing a letter, graphically
depict a tall building breaking and falling.
The horizontal 'terror' crossing the Key does so at the very point the
terrorists' airliner full of passengers crashed into the Tower (if pictured
here bottom to top).

Part 7 U.S. Wars

Afghanistan

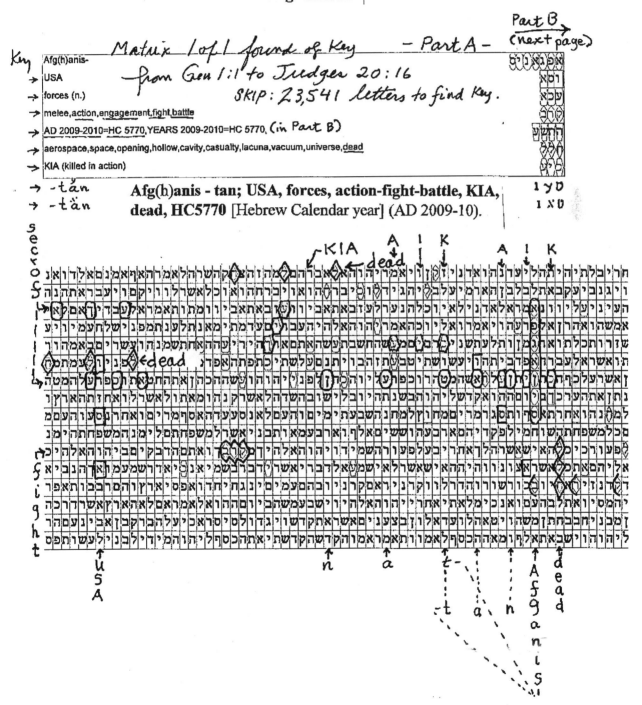

Key

Afg(h)anis-
USA
forces (n.)
melee,action,engagement,fight,battle
AD 2009-2010=HC 5770, YEARS 2009-2010=HC 5770, (in Part B)
aerospace,space,opening,hollow,cavity,casualty,lacuna,vacuum,universe,dead
KIA (killed in action)
-tăn
-tăn

Matrix 1 of 1 found of Key   — Part A —   Part B (next page)
from Gen 1:1 to Judges 20:16
SKIP: 23,541 letters to find Key.

Afg(h)anis - tan; USA, forces, action-fight-battle, KIA, dead, HC5770 [Hebrew Calendar year] (AD 2009-10).

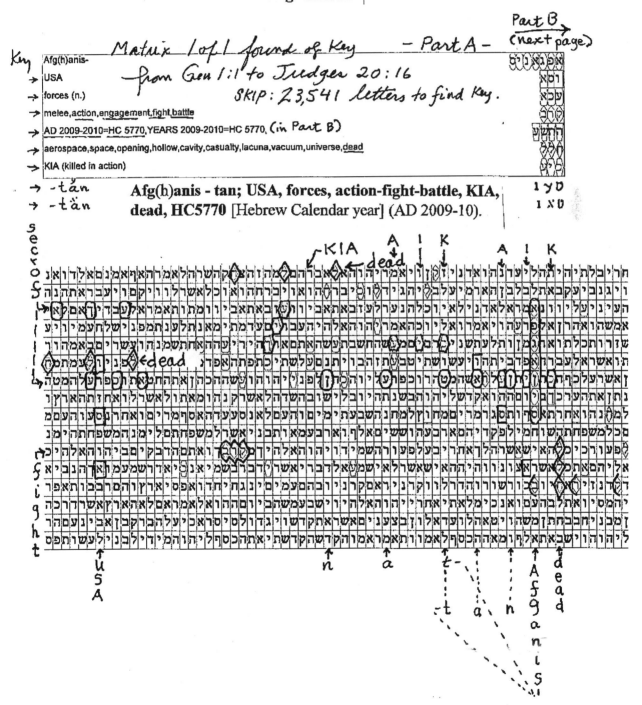

Part A
←

— Part B —

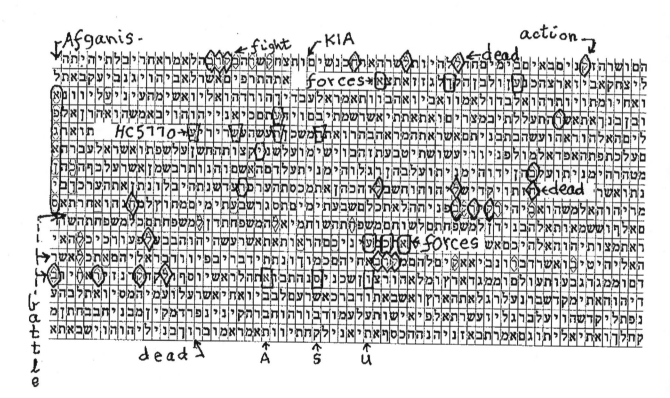

In the Proof-of-Concept Report available directly from the author, many names of the USA war dead, the full spelling of their names found Torah-encoded, are found encoded with this Key.

Gulf War

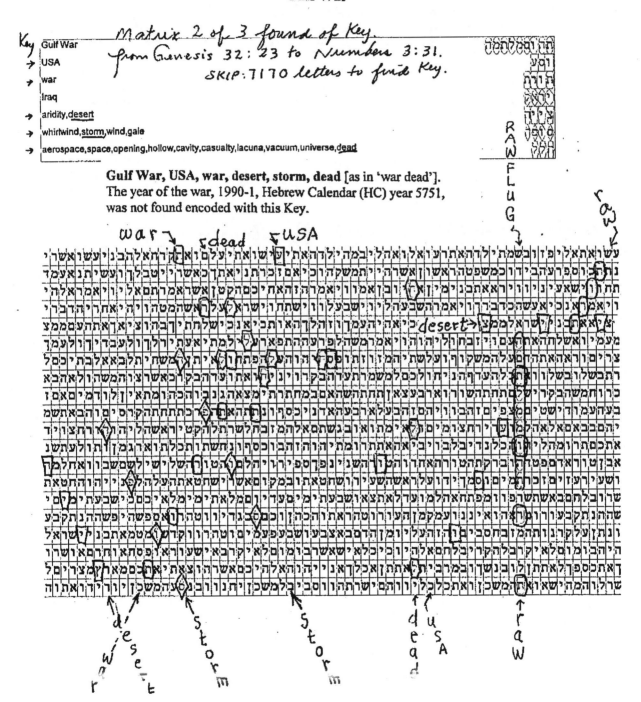

Matrix 2 of 3 found of Key.
from Genesis 32:23 to Numbers 3:31.
SKIP: 7170 letters to find Key.

Key:
- Gulf War
- → USA
- → war
- Iraq
- → aridity, desert
- → whirlwind, storm, wind, gale
- → aerospace, space, opening, hollow, cavity, casualty, lacuna, vacuum, universe, dead

Gulf War, USA, war, desert, storm, dead [as in 'war dead'].
The year of the war, 1990-1, Hebrew Calendar (HC) year 5751,
was not found encoded with this Key.

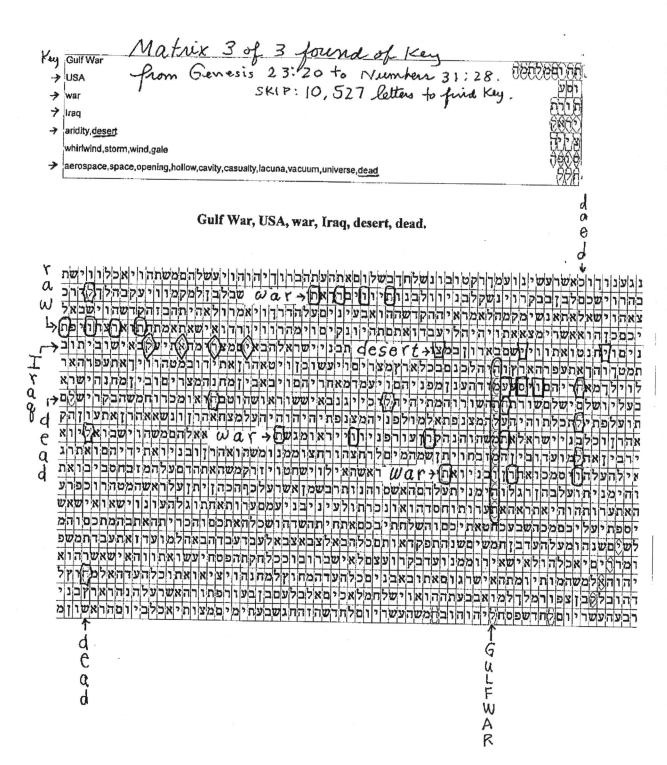

Gulf War, USA, war, Iraq, desert, dead.

Iraq War — "Desert Storm"

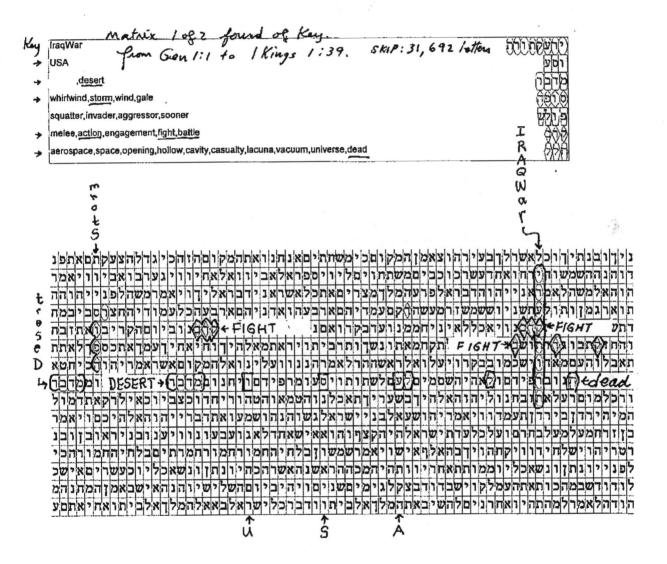

IraqWar, USA, action-engagement-fight-battle, Desert, Storm, dead.
That a 'fight-battle' in integrated in its encoded spelling with the Key is
significant, according to how such *proximity* shows relevance and
relatedness (see Satinover, and Sherman, in References).
[Part B shown in full Report, along with encoded names of U.S.
Troops who died].

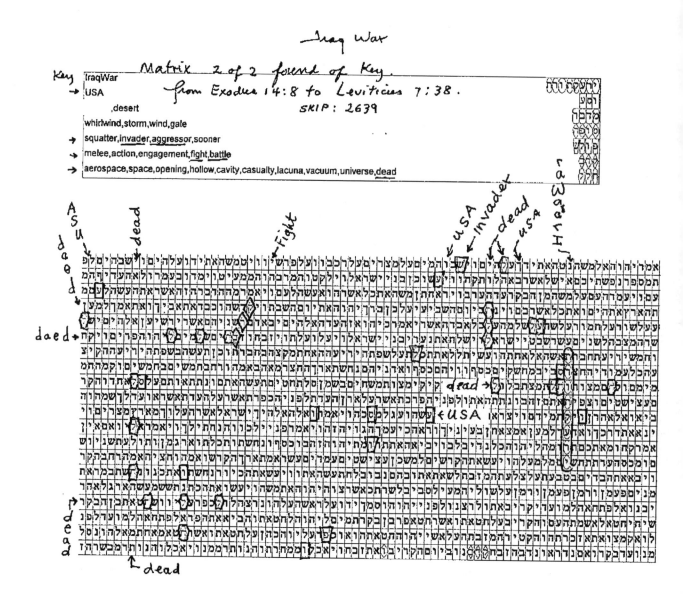

Iraq War

Matrix 2 of 2 found of Key.
from Exodus 14:8 to Leviticus 7:38.
SKIP: 2639

Key | IraqWar
→ USA
 ,desert
whirlwind,storm,wind,gale
→ squatter,invader,aggressor,sooner
→ melee,action,engagement,fight,battle
→ aerospace,space,opening,hollow,cavity,casualty,lacuna,vacuum,universe,dead

IraqWar, USA, invader, action-engagement-fight-battle, dead.
This is historically accurate in that the USA *was* the 'invader,' the encoded word of which only *one* was found in the 2 matrices for this Key, 'IraqWar' (composed of transliterated 'Iraq' combined with Hebrew word for 'war').
[Part B of this Matrix is shown in the full Report, along with the encoded names of the U.S. troops killed].

Vietnam

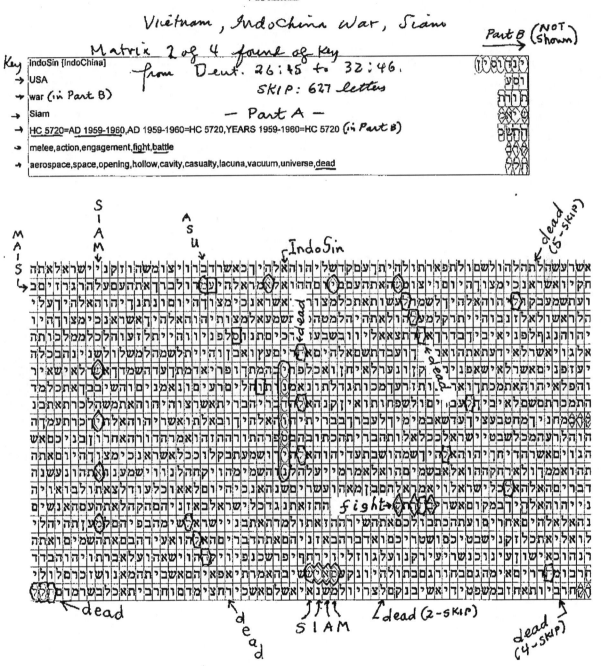

Vietnam, IndoChina War, Siam

Matrix 2 of 4 found of Key
from Deut. 26:45 to 32:46.
SKIP: 627 letters

— Part A —

Part B (NOT shown)

Key
→ IndoSin [IndoChina]
→ USA
→ war (in Part B)
→ Siam
→ HC 5720=AD 1959-1960,AD 1959-1960=HC 5720,YEARS 1959-1960=HC 5720 (in Part B)
→ melee,action,engagement,fight,battle
→ aerospace,space,opening,hollow,cavity,casualty,lacuna,vacuum,universe,dead

IndoSin, Siam, USA, War, fight/ba..., dead, HC5720 (1959-60).
In Hebrew 'China' is spelled 'Sin' (from the Bible Codes program's Lexicon).
Hebrew Calendar (HC) year 5720 corresponds to our Gregorian calendar, to part of 1959 and '60.
The war in IndoChina ('IndoSin', Siam, Vietnam) for the U.S. is dated by historians as starting in 1959, when President Eisenhower sent military advisors there, and ending in 1975 when President Nixon pulled all the troops out, in an agreement with the North Vietnamese that they soon violated, and took over the South. Henry Kissinger said he felt betrayed by the North in this.

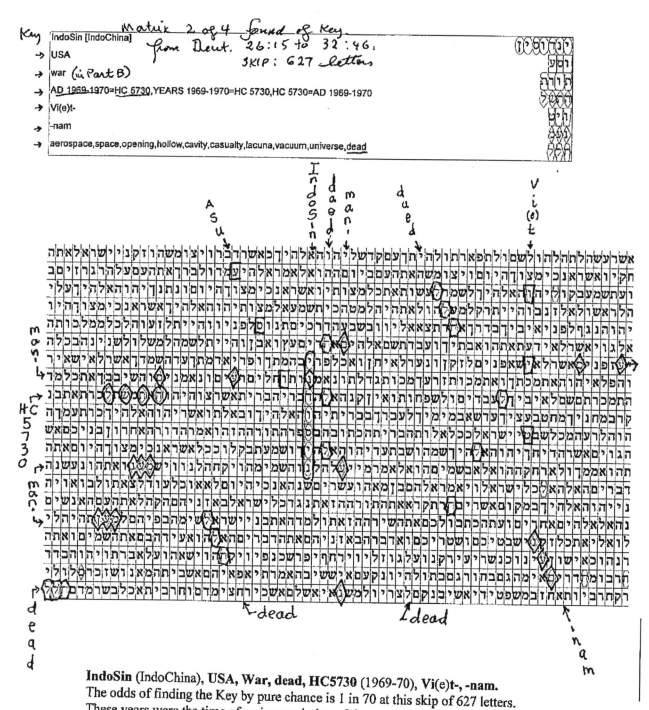

IndoSin (IndoChina), USA, War, dead, HC5730 (1969-70), Vi(e)t-, -nam.
The odds of finding the Key by pure chance is 1 in 70 at this skip of 627 letters.
These years were the time of major escalation of the war by the U.S.

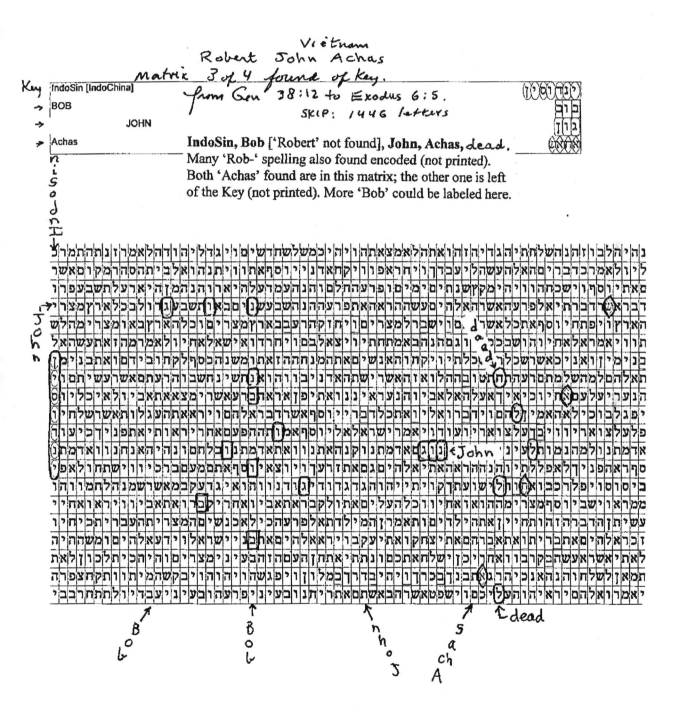

Vietnam
Robert John Achas
Matrix 3 of 4 found of Key.
from Gen 38:12 to Exodus 6:5.
SKIP: 1446 letters

IndoSin, Bob ['Robert' not found], **John, Achas,** *dead.*
Many 'Rob-' spelling also found encoded (not printed).
Both 'Achas' found are in this matrix; the other one is left
of the Key (not printed). More 'Bob' could be labeled here.

Part 8   World War Two City Bombings

Hiroshima

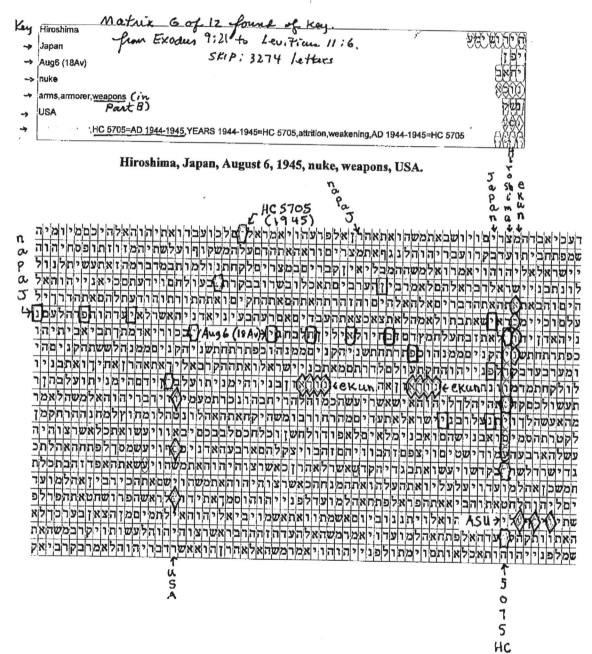

Key
- Hiroshima
- → Japan
- → Aug6 (18Av)
- → nuke
- → arms, armorer, weapons (in Part 8)
- → USA
- → HC 5705=AD 1944-1945, YEARS 1944-1945=HC 5705, attrition, weakening, AD 1944-1945=HC 5705

*Matrix 6 of 12 found of key.
from Exodus 9:21 to Leviticus 11:6.
SKIP: 3274 letters*

Hiroshima, Japan, August 6, 1945, nuke, weapons, USA.

Note Hebrew Calendar (HC) year <u>5705</u> (1945) is half-integrated into spelling of the Key, 'Hiroshima.' This goes beyond even the "proximity" significance (see Preface) and reveals the historically intimate nature of the event as what we might look at as 'inevitable,' as if the hands of fate were shaping the destiny of all factors surrounding this event. We are here trying to grasp and interpret, and still reflecting upon, some of the significance of such a Torah Code finding exposed in such a matrix as we see before us.

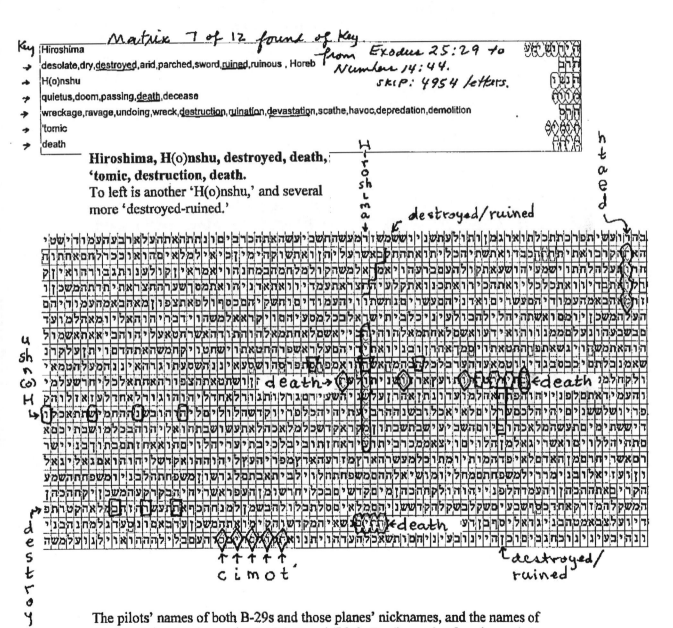

Key
Hiroshima
desolate,dry,destroyed,arid,parched,sword,ruined,ruinous , Horeb
H(o)nshu
quietus,doom,passing,death,decease
wreckage,ravage,undoing,wreck,destruction,ruination,devastation,scathe,havoc,depredation,demolition
'tomic
death

Matrix 7 of 12 found of Key from Exodus 25:29 to Numbers 14:44. Skip: 4954 letters.

Hiroshima, H(o)nshu, destroyed, death, 'tomic, destruction, death.
To left is another 'H(o)nshu,' and several more 'destroyed-ruined.'

The pilots' names of both B-29s and those planes' nicknames, and the names of the two A-bombs dropped ('Fat Man' and 'Little Boy') are also found encoded. See full Report, 90 pages long, in Book List for ordering information.

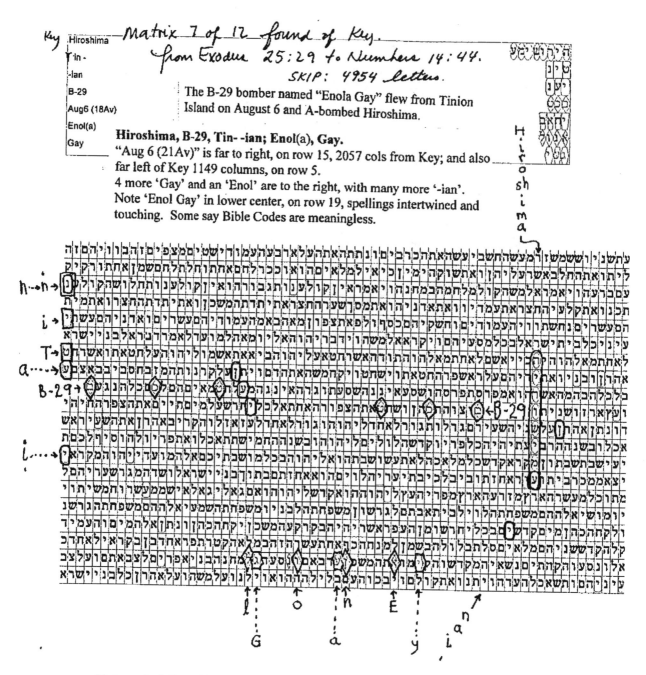

Matrix 7 of 12 found of Key.
from Exodus 25:29 to Numbers 14:44.
SKIP: 4954 letters.

The B-29 bomber named "Enola Gay" flew from Tinion Island on August 6 and A-bombed Hiroshima.

Hiroshima, B-29, Tin- -ian; Enol(a), Gay.
"Aug 6 (21Av)" is far to right, on row 15, 2057 cols from Key; and also far left of Key 1149 columns, on row 5.
4 more 'Gay' and an 'Enol' are to the right, with many more '-ian'.
Note 'Enol Gay' in lower center, on row 19, spellings intertwined and touching. Some say Bible Codes are meaningless.

Note on far left, spelling of 'Tinian' is on one column and shares a letter, 'n.'
Very near that is 'B-29,' which again is only 2 letters away from *another* '-ian,'
part of the island's name from which it took off very early in the morning of Aug. 6.
Note another 'B-29' is only 7 letters left of the Key, and the Key shares its 'a' with
a diagonal '-ian' – these 3 aspects of historical reality being so intimately entwined
we find such deliberate encoding of the truth by the Torah encoders.

Nagasaki

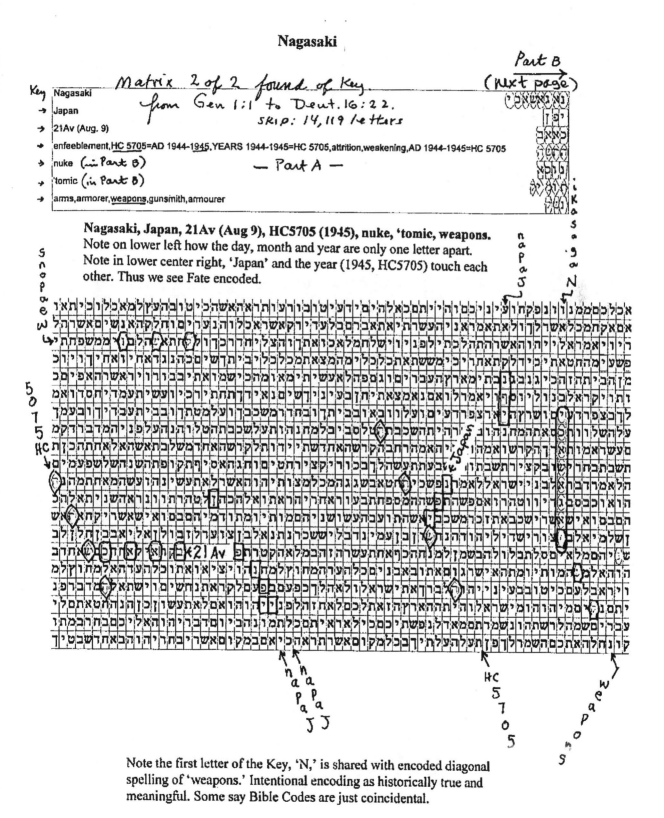

Nagasaki, Japan, 21Av (Aug 9), HC5705 (1945), nuke, 'tomic, weapons.
Note on lower left how the day, month and year are only one letter apart.
Note in lower center right, 'Japan' and the year (1945, HC5705) touch each
other. Thus we see Fate encoded.

Note the first letter of the Key, 'N,' is shared with encoded diagonal
spelling of 'weapons.' Intentional encoding as historically true and
meaningful. Some say Bible Codes are just coincidental.

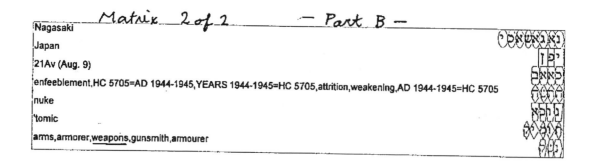

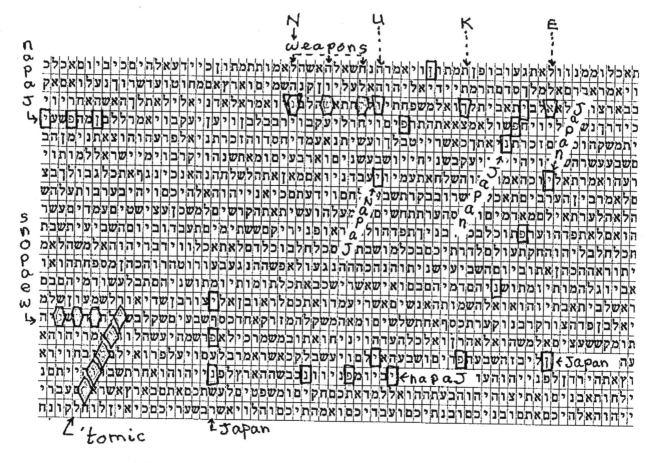

Note in lower left "'tomic" and 'weapons' are only 2 letters apart. Note in upper center, 'weapons' and 'nuke' share the Hebrew 'n', while 2 encoded diagonal 'Japan' cross the horizontal row on which 'nuke' and 'weapons' are found encoded and even integrated in their spellings. The information content here is descriptively and historically accurate and true. What more could we ask of this sacred text, even in its encoded form?

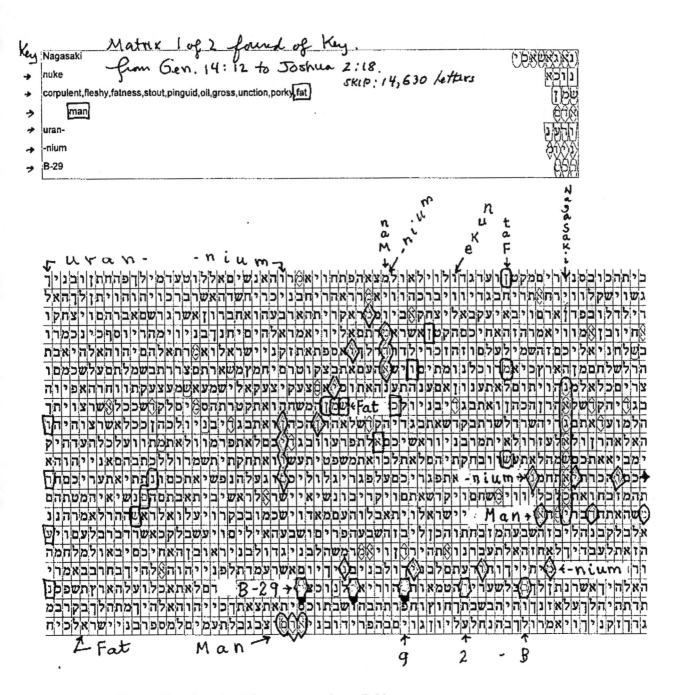

Matrix 1 of 2 found of Key.
from Gen. 14:12 to Joshua 2:18.
skip: 14,630 letters

Key
Nagasaki
→ nuke
→ corpulent,fleshy,fatness,stout,pinguid,oil,gross,unction,porky, fat
→ man
→ uran-
→ -nium
→ B-29

Nagasaki, nuke, Fat, Man, uran-, -nium; B-29.
The A-bomb dropped from the B-29 nicknamed "Bock's Car" was called
"Fat Man" (see photo elsewhere) and was a Uranium-239 bomb.
Hebrew words for "bomb, bombarding, and bombardment" weren't
found encoded with this Key.
Several more 'Fat,' 'Man,' and a '-nium' are found right of this screen print.

Afterword

"If our questions of [life and death] are to hold out the promise of self-knowledge that [birth itself has allowed for], we can't ask them outside of history." (See Gopnick, p.8).

Apparently the future has already been recorded, in a sacred text of 304,805 Hebrew letters, in the Torah. All of human history and events on the Earth are found encoded in the Books and verses from Genesis to Deuteronomy. Samples have been included in this volume.

This process presents us with an ethical conundrum of framing a relevant perspective that reveals a truth not immediately ready to disclose itself . . . illuminating the possibility of complex knowledge hidden in the mind of God that we can safely reveal in a format like this book—an exfoliation of evidence, perception and intuition . . . leading to a vibrant document, interpreting the evidence gleaned from the broken tongue of Yahweh.

Silent, we stand in awe, waiting for the next sky to fall, the next world to dissolve in an instant as we are transported to the eternal presence of the source of all Being, and again walk in a state of Grace.

This is God's Secret Code of Death embedded in the encrypted text of the sacred Torah, making the detective work itself a kind of sacred quest, a blessed calling, or at least a determined dedication of a sort of lone monk in the desert battling every day for a morsel of truth.

We the living bear witness to the vengeance, vengeance under the guise of blood cult sacrifice orchestrated by an agency beyond human comprehension, orchestrated by an intelligence beyond the strictures of time, and with the technical ability to encrypt a large text, the Torah made of 304,805 Hebrew letters, that apparently predicted the future as of about 3500 years ago. I Satinover (see References) cites conclusions by computer experts and the NSA that humans do not have at this time the ability to encrypt such a text to the deep extent as found in Bible Code research. He tells of NSA personnel, after delving into Bible Codes, taking early retirement and moving themselves and their families to Israel for further, deeper study.

We are witness to a secret on the tongue of God, a secret called Death. The celestial reckonings of the God of Death, meting out the mysterious justice of mortality in ways we never would in our blind ethics rendering the helpless and defenseless mere pawns in a king's whimsy of crass politics and the glory and survival of his people.

All human wars in recorded history—the dead named by God 3500 years ago. Later volumes in this series will search for those names in all the major wars and battles throughout human history, their full names to be found encoded in the Five Books of Moses. A few volumes now available in the Book List go some distance in fulfilling that goal.

How can we escape the naming, and thus perhaps escape death itself? In what sacred text prior to the Torah might be encoded the names of the dead in earlier wars, or are they also encoded in the Torah, and all we need to know are the names of those wars and battles? For example, in my book on **Assassinations,** ancient Egyptian names of those assassinated 4000 years ago were found encoded in the Torah (names known even before it was presented to the Hebrew people), as 'assassinated.'

Misplaced assumptions and unknown unknowns get in the way of creating clarity in our understanding of the necessary parameters for establishing knowledge in this enterprise. The causality issue is enlightening of what we don't know. Dissecting the matrix of space and time in order to tell the future exposes a utilitarian algorithm not used for centuries in the seance parlors of the spiritualist underworld.

Regarding terror attacks—among the top 31 terrorists in the world today, only one is a non-Muslim. An infidel is defined in Islam as any non-Muslim. A verse in the Koran says: "Kill the infidels wherever you find them." Muslims believe there are no innocent infidels, partly because if they were not anti-Muslim they would not be infidels, and since they have had opportunities to convert (three warnings are required in the Koran), their rejection is a constant reminder of their hostility to Islam and to the teachings of the Prophet (praise be upon him and his 9-year old, favorite wife, Aisha).

Moral equivalency of victims such as children, women and old men ignores intention—jihad terrorists aim for such civilians and hide among Muslim women and children, while the U.S. military aims at war targets and tries to avoid collateral civilian damage. Moral equivalency of "freedom fighter" and terrorist ignores the fact that terrorists don't believe in freedom as we understand it in Western civilization, and don't fight as such—setting IEDs and hiding among civilians to avoid battle engagement is not fighting in any traditional military sense.

"If your life is not on the line, it's not real." Factory Five spokesman; kit cars, 'Megakits,' 2011, on The Speed Channel.

The reality is that our lives are on the line every moment of every day, we just don't know what Key to look for in the Book of Death in order to tell when and where and how our number will be up. There may be a work-around that could potentially avoid that problem. The author is exploring various approaches to this problem.

The Torah is a text of coded secrets resulting in multi-dimensional Matrices when searched for connections and explanations of how to read reality. Although cracking open Joseph Chilton Pierce's "cosmic egg" might reveal a hidden reality of immeasurable scale, we are still left with our inescapable limitations restricting our assumptions about what is possible. Are we permitted to peer across the divide between living and dead?

Who will object to these findings and on what will those objections be based? The reaction of some is that these names of events, places and the dead, especially *all* these names, *should* not be found in small sections of the Torah, and *could* not reasonably be found encoded, much less found encoded closely bunched together around the 'Key' word, because such findings would be *far* beyond any reasonable expectation of chance, and thus would not be possible, based on a rational analysis of how language works.

Thus preconceived notions can create a blind spot of denial in which what is seen in black and white is not believed as true or as a legitimate outcome of a standard procedure in a research discipline that is about 900 years old. Objections within that field of investigation will come partly from rejecting the application of phonetic deconstruction of names into their syllables, as if the rule of meaningfulness from the phenomenon of observed *proximity* doesn't apply to those constituent parts of words uttered as whole sounds.

The dead are in the Word, their names broken within the encoded text, exactly as spoken on the broken tongue of Yahweh. Have the ancient encoders of that Sacred Word been able to break down the barrier not only of space and time but of consciousness and quantum being, focusing on an essence of humanity yet unidentified by us so far (leaving the question of 'soul' aside for now in our current effort to more clearly appraise our situation)?

The alphabet accommodates the tongue, so we see what is encoded in Holy Word when the tripping of the Sacred Tongue is phonetically and faithfully de-constructed to fit the ear of YHWH and the mouth of Moses.

Conclusion: Notes on Meaning

"Sometimes in order to see the light you have to risk the darkness."
(the inventor of Pre-Crime, in the movie "Minority Report," 2002)

As to the question, 'What does it mean?' I can only suggest I be invited to conduct a class or workshop or seminar to examine some of the preconceptions imbedded in such a question and look carefully and thoroughly at what would it mean for these discoveries to mean anything at all, taking into consideration an examination of *meaning* itself. Assuming that they do, we can explore the repercussions of the implications of what we might see implied here.

Confining our concerns to the meaning of these findings *qua* 'meaning' would be merely melodramatic. Through the Bible-Torah Code search process, applied to significant, historical events, we can curate them, synthesize the encoded data, and analyze the composite results, and finally put their implications in the context of the greater journey of humankind upon the Earth.

As Ogdon and Richards state in their 1923 Preface to their book *The Meaning of Meaning—A Study of the Influence of Language Upon Thought and of the Science of Symbolism*, "language is the most important of all the instruments of civilization." And thus we look through the lens of language in this Torah Code mystery to try and understand what it means to be human.

Bertrand Russell, on page 47 of his *Principles of Mathematics*, says: "Words all have meaning, in the simple sense that they are symbols which stand for something other than themselves . . . . Thus meaning, in the sense in which words have meaning, is irrelevant to logic." (See p.273 of Ogdon and Richards).

In an attempt at meta-understanding of the meaning of what is found encoded in the Torah, we can begin to appreciate the layers of language embedded within language that hold long-standing truths bursting at the proverbial seams to break free and announce themselves in a song of deeper understanding of what drips from the broken tongue of Yahweh. Gathered here we have presented some samples of that potential in hopes of them shedding light on what is possible to understand of what is secretly buried inside this sacred text.

"The odds against chance are dropping fast."
Jack (Harrison Ford) in movie, *Patriot Games* (1992)

Calculating the probability of finding all these encoded terms close to each other and in *one* Matrix, and all close to the Key (multiply each successive probability with each other to find out what the odds are against pure chance; will be exceedingly small), shows an exponential decrease against chance each time we find such Torah search results. Coincidence plays an increasingly smaller role as we continue to explore this phenomenon of encoded historical secrets. Satinover points out that Torah Code researchers have concluded that the encoding of the text was not only far beyond chance but was done *intentionally.*

"The connection between the calligraphy and the sword is a mystery. The mystery can be explained only by those who can perceive the connection between them." (Martial arts master Jet Li, Master Lin the assassin, in Chinese movie *Hero*, 2002, directed by Zhang Yimou, who also directed "Raise the Red Lantern").

Not only has the connection been explained by the author, but the demonstrably valid conclusion can be drawn based on the explained connection (between Hebrew in the Torah [the calligraphy] and murder [the sword]) that God is not squeamish.

"The gods are worthless as protectors." ('Snow' to the assassin, Jet Li). 'The brush and the sword share the same principles." (Brother Sword to Snow). So the Word and Death share the same principles, are intuitively connected through tongue, breath and mortality.

"Men and sword become interchangeable." (The King to Master Lin, Jet Li). "A warrior's ultimate act is to lay down his sword." (Master Lin to the King after he stabs him from behind with the king's sword).

The Glory of the Word becomes a Death Nell for those enshrined in the Death Matrix of the Holy text. Only non-identity could save any of us from that fate, but since even DNA is the essence of individual identity that can be delineated and transliterated into corresponding Hebrew letters in proper sequence (A-T, G-C) in full expression for individual identification, there is no escape along that front. We realize there is no escape from Yahweh already having called us to oblivion. The only differentiating factor is timing, the when of the end, and that is unknown and cannot be predicted with much degree of certainty. Even suicides are not always successful. Yahweh's prohibition against people trying to see into the future is spelled out in Deuteronomy 18: 10-14. Given the modern superstitious mind-set, it is worth reading.

How do we explain this Bible Code phenomenon? Edward O. Wilson has argued that "there is intrinsically only one class of explanation. It traverses the scales of space, time, and complexity to unite the disparate facts of the disciplines of consilience, the perception of a seamless web of cause and effect." (on p.266 of his 1998 book *Consilience: the Unity of Knowledge*).

If I could repeal the encoded Word of God, I would, but His will cannot be avoided, negated, countered or neutralized, so the carnage among humans will continue. YHWH long ago tried to wipe all humans off the surface of the Earth through the flooding power of the Deluge, the Great Flood. After this attempt failed, Yahweh promised not to use water again to try and kill all humans. What purpose, in YHWH's mind, does a "flood of blood" serve? Is it a substitute for a "flood of water" but still vengeance upon humanity for continuing to offend YHWH in some way, perhaps just by existing?

Genesis 6-9 tells the Deluge story of the Great Flood, a devastating worldwide catastrophe that occurred in about 2348 BC, according to one calculation (see Wikipedia). While apparently intended by YHWH as a prelude to a new beginning for mankind, according to one interpretation explaining why Noah and his family were saved, in order to re-populate the Earth. But Noah was not warned by Yahweh of the coming Deluge, nor did Yahweh instruct him how to build the Ark—a voice behind a wall did that (see Sitchin for the identity of who that was). And repopulating the Earth would not be possible from such a small genetic base as only one family, even if incest were sanctioned and encouraged.

Epilogue: 2 poems for the dead

Poem

Trust not the truth that
comes from afar
a smile tinged as a masked
doubt, a foundling at the
door of death

The gap between tongues
everlasting throughout history
quells any desire to sink dreams,
vapid hopes built on false assumptions,
indulgences that lead to a dark river

Built on hope and rumors meant to
bring down enterprise and erase profit
hidden as sacred breath we share,
bury ourselves in the mystery,
the answers run pure and final

Poem

The blade of universal time
cuts both ways
the pendulum of the heart
settles the score

As mundane concerns of a grieving monk
bespeak truth twisted as lies,
moments sacrificed and
desires evaporated

With none of the schoolgirl contrivances
deployed to examine available quandaries
wrapped in extra hair,
extra looks and exhausted quiverings

Now part of the landfill
her arms around it
just below the skin

(The author's dozens of published poems have appeared in literary journals for 45 years, in 5 countries, such as 5 poems in *The Paris Review,* 1971 and 1972; and with at least one Nobel Prize winner for Literature, Pablo Neruda, the Chilean poet).

Appendix

Calendar Adjustment is Needed to Correct the Gregorian Calendar in use Worldwide Today

While this section is sparsely sourced, information on how and why the Gregorian Calendar we use needs adjustment due to our lack of knowledge about what year Jesus was born is readily available to those with the right research tools. Further references and sources provided to the author would be much appreciated—contact at scanada@webtv.net, subject line: 'GregCalAdj;' but this email service stops on Sept. 30, 2013, so please use postal mail after that date.

The Gregorian Calendar is a modified version of the Julian Calendar. It is also called the Western calendar and the Christian calendar, and is the most internationally widely accepted and used civil calendar; see Wikipedia.com. In 1582 the Julian Calendar was changed to the Gregorian Calendar, and adopted in 1752 in England, Scotland and the colonies. In 45 B.C. Julius Caesar ordered a calendar consisting of 12 months based on a solar year. This calendar employed a cycle of three years of 365 days, followed by a year of 366 days (leap year); see www.cslib.org/calendar; Conn State Library.

Also see www.webexhibits.org; ("How did Dionysius date Christ's birth? Was Jesus born in year 0)?" Also see www.johnpratt.com ("Gregorian Calendar calculated the year of Christ's birth from the available records . . ."). Also: www.new-birth.net ("The likely dates of Jesus' birth and death; born probably on Wednesday, Jan. 7, 7 BC; died probably on Friday, March 8, 29 AD"). Also: www.calendersign.com; and www.Suite101.com ("the year of Jesus' birth").

It's a popular misconception, based on an anti-historical and inti-intellectual stance that we can't look at the past to learn about the future. Hasn't that been one of the main source of resistance to using the Bible Codes, whose sources are literally thousands of years old? The work required to frame our understanding of the past, in the discipline of History, for example, is not an easy or obvious fit to how we extend that understanding into how we see the future.

Futurism and future history get confused with each other, and many people want to opt out of trying to comprehend the implications of either the past and how it has shaped our present, and how that present formulates our launch from here into an unknown, perhaps even unknowable, at least for some, future. How do we resist our destiny? Should we? Should we embrace our fate and trust whoever is in control?

Even trying to coordinate the calendar with events that occur and events seemingly predicted in the Bible can be problematical as to the year we're talking about, since the Gospels make no mention of a year or a time when Jesus was born. The question of what year especially has been a matter of intense debate, because our Gregorian Calendar is supposed to begin with the first full year of Jesus' life. How might we reconcile this?

The first full year of Jesus' life was fixed as the first year of our calendar by the monk and Vatican scholar Dionysius Exiguss. One day he counted 525 years from his present time (which he knew as year 248 during the Diocletian Era) to the year of the incarnation and birth of Jesus. He then reset that year as year 1 'Ante Christum Natum' ('before the birth of Christ'), 1 ACN, or BC for short. This dating system came to be universally accepted in the 8th century, and we still use it today.

So how do we really know what year it is, in order to see any encoded year in the Bible Code Matrices in context to a time-line we can get a firm handle on?

The Gospels are problematic because they offer two accounts that chronologists find incompatible. Matthew 2:16 states that Jesus was born while Herod the Great was still alive and that Herod ordered the slaughter of infants two years old and younger, and based on the date of Herod's death in 4 BC (contra Dionysius Exiguss), many chronologists conclude that the year 6 BC is the most likely year of Jesus' birth. Consequently, Jesus would have been about four to six years old in the year AD 1.

While we know that Christ was born quite some time before 1 BC, we need to keep in mind that Herod the Great died in 4 BC, so for him to have played such a large role in the event surrounding Jesus' birth, tied as it is to the 'Massacre of the Innocents,' these events must have taken place before or during 4 BC. We can, by the way, be certain of Herod's death by dating the lunar eclipse that occurred right before, as asserted by the first century historiographer Josephus. But that only gives us the year at the *latest*. If we take the Star of Bethlehem as the conjunction of Jupiter and Saturn, then Jesus could have been born even earlier, in 8 BC.

So we cannot with precision know the timing of any event referred to in the Bible Codes that are presented in the Matrix search findings? If our calendar is wrong, how do we know when any particular event happened? Just arbitrarily adjust it within a range of years we can estimate as the birth year of Jesus? That would not make for very accurate history.

Unfortunately, one of the more historically precise indications we have to go on, namely Luke's reference to Quirinius' census, conflicts with Josephus' statement that Quirinius was indeed governor and that there was indeed a census, but in 6 AD, long after Herod's death.

Is there any way we can see to build accuracy into this data that would make it more useful to us in trying to anticipate what is to come? I guess we could keep adding or subtracting years to any found encoded year, and add vigilance during those times.

Before I agree with that approach to dealing with the future with uncertainty, which will probably turn out to be the most useful on a practical basis, although potentially stressful and draining of options, let me recap the telling point here about the calendar. On the one hand, Luke's account places Jesus' birth during a census conducted under the governorship of Quirinius, who according to Josephus, conducted a census in AD 6. In order to reconcile the two Gospel accounts, some have suggested that Josephus was mistaken or that Quirinius had a separate period of rule under Herod. In any case, the actual date of his birth remains historically unverifiable. We will probably never know for certain when Christ was born, or for that matter, when he died on the cross.

We can work out later how such figuring can fit into the Code research results found. But how do we fight the future? If there is a way to fight it, what might that be? Knowledge about what is coming would increase our chances for long-term survival as a species. As for trusting whoever is in control (if there actually is such a mechanism), whatever is coming in our future has already apparently been encoded in the holy script we've talked about. Uncovering it with some degree of accuracy would give us a leg up on options for survival.

In other words, knowing what to anticipate would give us a fighting chance to possibly effectively resist the will behind the intentional actions portrayed in the encoded Torah. While the Books and Reports listed at the end of this book (and other planned by the author) illuminate the fact that the secretly encoded Torah apparently holds the whole history of humanity within its 304,805 Hebrew letters, arranged in an encrypted way far beyond any human capacity to encode (per Jeffrey Satinover, MD, 1997, a reference used in all of the author's Bible Code volumes; see for example one of his 15 websites: www.PredictingPresidents.com, in which all U.S. presidents' elections' outcomes can be predicted using two search result factors detected by the author), we might not be limited to looking at only the past if an effective algorithm can be developed to in effect program the Torah's text to look into the future, that is, decode it in a way that introduces the dimension of time into a 3-dimensionally configured matrix. Such attempts to look into the future would not violate YHWH's injunction listed in Deuteronomy 18: 10-14.

References

Gopnik, Adam, 2011, *The Table Comes First: Family, France, and the Meaning of Food*, Knopf.

C.K. Ogdon and I.A. Richards, 1923, *The Meaning of Meaning,* reissued 1989, NY: HBJ.

Satinover, Jeffrey, MD, 1997, *Cracking the Bible Code*, NY: Quill-HarperCollins.

Sherman, R. Edwin, 2004, *Bible Code Bombshell*, Bloomington, IN: Author House.

Sitchin, Zecharia, 1978, *The 12thPlanet*, NY: Avon; and his other 5 books in the *Earth Chronicles* series.

Wilson, Edward O., 1998, *Consilience: the Unity of Knowledge*, NY: Knopf.

About the Author

An Army brat born in Maine in1941, he was educated in 3 states and five countries, including later at Uppsala University, Sweden, and Alliance Francaise, Paris, France. He now lives deep in the California desert, having retired early from a coastal county's Social Services department, and devotes himself full time to writing—dozens of books on deciphering crop circles since 1990, and dozens of poems published in literary journals in 5 countries since 1968. He taught school (maths and science) in northern England 1967-68, and has degrees in Sociology. Divorced in1975, San Francisco; no children.

He has conducted college and university extension workshops in Massachusetts and California 1988-1998, including on writing poetry; given public lectures on his crop circle decipherment findings and theory throughout California and in Tucson, Arizona; been interviewed on Fox-TV's "Encounters" (1995), and on TV affiliate in Santa Maria, California, cable access TV in Santa Barbara, and cable access TV in Tucson ("The Cutting Edge," in 2004 and 2005). Also interviewed on various radio shows (local, regional, and Canadian), including "Coast to Coast" in mid-December, 2000.

More recently, his interest in Bible Codes has resulted in a series of dozens of self-published books. He is a member of the "Isaac Newton Bible Code Research Society," located in southern Oregon, founded by R. Edwin Sherman.

Books and Reports List

Confidential Report and Book series in which names of victims of accidents, natural disasters, holocausts, mass shootings, assassinations, terror attacks, and wars are shown found encoded in the Torah. All are 8.5 x 11" size, velo or spiral bound; shipping is included in price for each. Send check or money order (in USD only please) to author, Steve Canada, at 1123 N. Las Posas, Ridgecrest, CA 93555, USA.

1. **Concordia Cruise Ship Disaster**—All Victims' Names Found Encoded. (about 80pp, $29).
2. **Titanic's Sinking** and All Victim's Names Found Encoded. (about 200pp, $65).
3. **Assassinations Worldwide** Found Torah-Encoded: 4000 Years, over 5 Continents; samples, not exhaustive, but many with assassins' name, the location and year . . . including John Lennon (about 160pp, $52).
4. **Nazi Holocaust** Torah Codes—Death Camps and Victims' Names found encoded. This is a proof-of-concept manuscript; at one name per page for matrix-encoded, it would take over 6 million pages for an exhaustive illustrated presentation. If anyone knows of a publisher willing to take on such a project, please have them contact the author; (206pp; $65).
5. **Sandy Hook** Elementary School Shooting, Newtown, Conn., Dec. 14, 2012—All Victims' Names and the Shooter's, and his mother's, and the weapon, found Torah-encoded; including the psychology of *why* (matricide, homicide, rage, hatred); (65pp, $24).
6. **Five Other Mass Shootings**: collected between two covers—all victims and the shooters at Aurora, Columbine, Kent State, Santa Monica, and Tucson (about 96 pages, $34).
7. **Earthquakes: "temblors"**—proof-of-concept manuscript, only *some* of the thousands of pages that could be generated; book publishing contract with a publisher sought; (50pp, $20).
8. **Fukushima**: earthquake, tsunami, and nuclear power plant meltdown, March 2011 found Torah-encoded; only 14 victims' names, of the thousands, were found online; (106pp, $35).

9. **Hurricanes in U.S.**—proof-of-concept manuscript only, that is, only *some* of the thousands of pages that could be generated; book publishing contract with a publisher sought; (50pp, $20).

10. **Tornadoes in U.S.;** proof-of-concept book only, that is, only *some* of the many thousands of pages that could be generated showing the dead encoded in the Torah; (50pp, $20).

11. **Tsunamis;** proof-of-concept book only; hundreds of thousands have died worldwide over the years, so once their names are known, many thousands of pages could be generated as those names are found encoded in the Torah; (50pp, $20).

12. **Volcanos;** proof-of-concept book; only *some* of the names that could be found encoded in the Torah once their names are known; publisher and research assistant sought; (50pp, $20).

13. **9/11 Terror Attack, Twin Tower, NYC;** victims' names found Torah-encoded; proof-of-concept book, only *some* of the nearly 2800 victims' names are presented here (100pp, $35). A publishing contract would result in *all* names being shown as Torah-encoded, with the name of the event as the Key. Pentagon and Shanksville, Penn. victims would be done later, with a book publishing contract.

14. **Benghazi, Boston and Fort Hood**; 3 Terror Attacks combined between 2 covers; all names of victims shown Torah-encoded, along with the attackers'; (about 50pp, $20).

15. **Afghanistan War**: U.S. Troop Casualties Names; proof-of-concept (about 100pp, $35).

16. **The Gulf War**: U.S. Troop Casualties' Names found encoded; proof-of-concept (84pp, $29).

17. **Iraq War: "Desert Storm"**—U.S. Troop Casualties' Names found Torah encoded; proof-of-concept book (80pp, $29). Later, "Operation Iraqi Freedom," and "Operation Enduring Freedom" could be done as full-length books, with a publishing contract from a book publisher.

18. **Vietnam War**; U.S. Casualties' Names found in Torah Codes; proof-of-concept; 185pp, $59.

19. **WWII City Bombings: Hiroshima and Nagasaki**; atomic bombings of Japan found Torah-encoded; no names available anywhere, except on the two memorials at locations, in Japan only; public appeal for names announced here; all other factors found encoded, including the two B-29 nicknames, and both pilots' names, and even the island from where they took off; 90pp, $32.

Other, Planned Bible Death Code Books by Author:

1. <u>Korean War</u>: U.S. Troop Casualties; later volumes to include South Korean troops, other United Nations troops such as Turkey, North Korean troops, and Chinese troops in the war, 1950-53; and pilots on both sides, including U.S., Chinese, Russian, and North Korean.
2. <u>World War Two</u>: troops on all sides in both theaters, in ground, naval, and air campaigns.
3. <u>World War One</u>: troops on all sides, in ground, naval, and air campaigns.
4. <u>U.S. Civil War</u>: troops on both sides.
5. <u>Mexican-American War</u>: troops on both sides.
6. <u>Spanish-American War</u>: troops on both sides.
7. <u>War of 1812</u>: troops on both sides.
8. <u>American Revolutionary War</u>: troops on both sides.
9. <u>Peloponnesian War</u>: troops on both sides.
10. Other Mass Shootings in U.S., such as <u>Virginia Tech</u>, and the <u>Valentine's Day Massacre</u>.
11. Mass Shootings in other countries throughout history, such as <u>Germany</u> (worst school shooting in history), and in <u>Norway</u> (Andres Breivik on gun-free zone island where he shot 77 young campers and their counselors in 2011); Beslan, <u>Russia</u>, school siege by Chechen rebels, 334 hostages killed, including 186 children.